Designing Composite Applications

 PRESS

SAP PRESS is issued by
Bernhard Hochlehnert, SAP AG

SAP PRESS is a joint initiative of SAP and Galileo Press. The know-how offered by SAP specialists combined with the expertise of the publishing house
Galileo Press offers the reader expert books in the field. SAP PRESS features
first-hand information and expert advice, and provides useful skills for professional decision-making.

SAP PRESS offers a variety of books on technical and business related topics
for the SAP user. For further information, please visit our website:
www.sap-press.com.

Jo Weilbach, Mario Herger
SAP xApps and the Composite Application Framework
2005, 293 pp., ISBN 1-59229-048-5

Steffen Karch, Loren Heilig et al.
SAP NetWeaver Roadmap
2005, 312 pp., ISBN 1-59229-041-8

Chris Whealy
Inside Web Dynpro for Java
A guide to the principles of programming in SAP's Web Dynpro
2005, 356 pp., ISBN 1-59229-038-8

Arnd Goebel, Dirk Ritthaler
SAP Enterprise Portal
Technology and programming
2005, 310 pp., ISBN 1-59229-018-3

Jörg Beringer, Karen Holtzblatt

Designing Composite Applications

Driving user productivity and business information
for next generation business applications

 PRESS

Editor Florian Zimniak
Copy Editor Nancy Etscovitz, UCG, Inc.,
Boston, MA
Cover Design Silke Braun
Printed in Germany

ISBN 1-59229-065-5

Contents

3 Requirements Gathering 63

4 Seeing the Big Picture 89

5 Designing with Building Blocks 111

Back in the 90s, Contextual Design helped SAP to improve the usability of business applications by understanding individual user needs and work practice. Contextual interviews became a standard technique for gathering user-centered requirements and analyzing work group collaboration.

Contextual Design captures in-depth knowledge of the context in which products will be used, a critical pre-requisite to deliver products that provide high value and are intuitive to use. Insights gained from Contextual Design Work Models last far beyond one particular development project or product release. They can be used to improve products by renewing them—leaving their essence intact, but strengthening them substantially, or by driving product innovation.

Heinz Roggenkemper,
EVP of Business Process Renovation, SAP Labs, Palo Alto

Being a pilot customer for SAP xApps was a win-win opportunity. The process of understanding business needs, and ultimately functional requirements, was facilitated through Contextual Design activities, such as interviews conducted in the user's daily work environment and later through prototype feedback sessions. This user-focused approach enabled SAP to gain direct insight into business drivers, and it challenged us to push beyond the status quo and think about better ways of working.

Once delivered, the solutions provided capabilities that crossed traditional functional lines; a good example is xPD (xApp Product Definition), which draws together users from multiple business areas to develop product concepts. With the rapid maturing of the NetWeaver platform, we are looking forward to the prospect of a rich set of business integration, and analytics services that xApps can utilize.

xApp Pilot Customer

About This Book

The design of business applications is undergoing a major paradigm shift; with new technologies and new demands, business can drive innovation into their organizations reliably. Enterprise resource planning (ERP) applications used to be focused on transactional data processing and process consistency, and designed to support trained professional users. Today, core ERP processes are automated and streamlined. The bulk of the work of running businesses has shifted to information workers challenged to find the information they need to support decision-making and ad-hoc exception handling. Modern business applications can improve business efficiency by enhancing the productivity of these individuals and their collaboration within their work groups.

Technologies, like the SAP NetWeaver business process platform, help the enterprise run its traditional business processes, identify new opportunities, and quickly adapt to changes. The core platform secures the ongoing business, but composite applications built on top of the platform address the need for improvements and new opportunities. Composite applications require an application development framework to orchestrate platform services into modern business solutions. SAP® xApps™ built on the SAP NetWeaver® platform and the SAP Composite Application Framework (CAF) are SAP's first products delivering the technology required to support the development of modern business applications.[1]

But technology alone is not sufficient. Successful business applications must also address the experience of its users. Applications will not be adopted and new processes will not be implemented if they don't work for both the business *and* the user. Next-generation composite applications that support users, their work groups, and enterprise processes can offer productivity tools and collaboration in the context of business processes. These applications require a robust requirements

---

1 For more information on SAP NetWeaver and related technologies, go to *www.sdn.sap.com.*

gathering and design process to ensure that the needs of both users and business processes are supported. SAP xApps can deliver a more goal-oriented user experience aligned with business objectives while leveraging SAP's new technology for optimal use.

This book introduces the concepts of composite application development and an associated user-centered design process streamlined to support the development of composite applications. We adapt the Contextual Design[2] method, a well-established customer-centered design process used by companies and taught in universities all over the world, to the needs of creating a better user experience in business applications based on reusable user experience building blocks in the SAP NetWeaver platform. Contextual Design (CD) is grounded in ethnographic studies of the user and business process, represents the data in appropriate work models, and develops the design through early prototypes tested with users in the field.

Throughout the book, we provide you with selected examples of an SAP xApp™ product development project: The SAP xApp Product Definition (SAP xPD) is an SAP xApp supporting collaborative idea generation and requirements management within a product innovation context. Understanding the user-centered design techniques of Contextual Design and the user experience building blocks provided with the SAP NetWeaver platform, you can start quickly on the road to packaged composite applications development.

Audience

This book is for anyone developing composite applications that can take advantage of modern business platform technologies. Contextual Design is a team-based process that brings together all who are responsible for the development to create a shared understanding of users' needs, process redesign, and ultimate system design. This book is relevant to marketing, product management, UI designers, developers, and usability professionals developing a business solution for a

---

2 For more information on Contextual Design and InContext services, go to *www.incontextdesign.com.*

market or for a specific customer. It is also relevant to business analysts, process engineers, developers, and usability professionals developing composite applications for internal business use.

Acknowledgements

We wish to thank all those people whose hard work went into the creation of this book. Thanks to the SAP xPD team for using the Contextual Design method and for producing a successful application that we can use as an example. We also want to thank the SAP xApp design group for providing input and snapshots of the actual design process. We especially want to thank Hugh Beyer, a wonderful writer and co-founder of the Contextual Design process, for his writing, editing, and negotiating support, without whom this book would not exist.

Introduction

Enterprise applications are in a state of crisis. The demands of businesses on IT groups have never been greater. The intense pace of competition that comes with globalization is forcing businesses to look for improvements in every process that they implement and in every project that they undertake. Yet the techniques available for developing systems have not grown with the demand. Consequently, IT groups are getting further and further behind. "Whatever you recommend," we were told on one reengineering project recently, "just remember, the IT group has a four-year backlog."

But now new systems concepts and new technology are ready to transform enterprise systems development. This book introduces the composite application development paradigm, supported by new technology that is now available. The SAP service-oriented business process platform promises to radically reduce development delivery times and dramatically simplify the work of defining, designing, and delivering an enterprise-level application

What kind of problems beg for this new approach? Consider the following examples:

▶ In 1997, the Kyoto Protocol imposed new constraints on industrial emissions. National governments are responding with new emissions control and monitoring regulations and your company will have to conform. How quickly can you develop systems that help people track emissions, report on them, and identify and respond to deviations, without having to disrupt legacy systems and integrate these new systems with existing work systems?

▶ You're in the business of producing a consumer product—hair dryers. In this commodity market, it's critical that you can identify an unmet need, invent a new product concept to address that need, and get the product on store shelves quickly, that is, within 3–6 months. Yet the whole process of product concept development is unarticulated and unsupported. The business needs a system to help manage product concepts—the generation, development, and evaluation of these concepts, culminating in moving promising concepts to product development. You need a solution fast. How quickly can you respond? (Hint: "Four years is *not* a good answer.")

Why are these hard problems? Introducing new systems and business processes into the complex environment of a modern business is a challenge. The risks are large—most companies depend on critical legacy systems that must not be disrupted. Companies have layers of support and management software in place, supporting highly complex business processes. And—as always—they are broken down into multiple cooperating and competing silos that somehow get the work done.

Furthermore, many of the new opportunities are of the sort characterized by our two examples: They seek to leverage strategic, collaborative, decision-making processes characterized by a high degree of communication across traditional silos. This is a new breed of application that is expanding the scope of automation in the enterprise.

Businesses *must* introduce new systems to respond to external changes and internal goals. An effective approach for developing applications is desperately needed. This approach must be flexible enough to deal with the range of challenges and rapid changes facing business today. It must be powerful enough to support the new kinds of solutions businesses need. And it must support the teams and work groups that make business happen without disrupting the systems and processes that are already in place.

Science fiction? No, the technology is available today, but technology alone is not sufficient. With this book, you'll learn how to discover and define the needs of the business, assemble the components of a coherent solution, integrate legacy databases and systems, and provide the user with an integrated environment in which to work—all based on tested and proven design principles, and all at the speed necessary to serve today's business.

This approach to design is based on three fundamental concepts: *packaged composite applications*, *user-centered design*, and *development with*

UI building blocks. So let's take a moment to introduce these concepts and describe how they fit together to make up a solution to our problem.

Packaged Composite Applications

Packaged composite applications (PCAs) describe the new kind of applications we are focusing on in this book. Rather than attempting to design and deploy a new system as a self-contained whole, PCAs view the new system as an organic extension of a system platform that already exists.

If we take the term apart, we're talking about *applications* that:

▶ Provide new functionality that goes beyond simply integrating existing systems

▶ Expand support to flexible, configurable, collaborative processes that go beyond the scope of existing applications

▶ Allow analysis followed by action, exceeding read-only aggregation of corporate information

They are *composite* because they:

▶ Aggregate functionality of existing systems, as exposed through Web services

▶ Cross traditional application boundaries

▶ Create a comprehensive process and information model

And being *packaged* results in:

▶ Products with a lower total cost of ownership (TCO) than custom development

▶ Products with integration costs leveraged over a large customer base

▶ Products supported with new releases and maintenance

In other words, a PCA is an application that uses underlying enterprise services to unlock the value of a company's existing systems. It gathers the information from all the heterogeneous legacy applications into a unified, homogenous form, and then uses that information to build a new, focused solution based on a comprehensive view of the enterprise.[1]

This new application paradigm offers a way around the roadblocks that typically hamper the design, development, and introduction of new systems. Composite applications build on (legacy) systems rather than replacing them; work across silos, providing overall monitoring and cross-departmental coordination; and are especially strong in extending automation to new areas such as decision support and strategic systems.

But a "paradigm" isn't enough. You can't generate a new enterprise application with a paradigm. The industry needs concrete development platforms that instantiate this paradigm—that make it possible to design and develop composite applications for real-life systems.

That's where the SAP business process platform comes in. SAP NetWeaver provides tools and services that make it easy to build packaged composite applications like SAP xApps, which package new process support and improved user experience with flexible back-end links to legacy and new data stores. Rather than treating every project as a new problem, composite applications build in a number of well-understood process patterns and user interface paradigms, ready for you to tailor to help you resolve your business problem.

The collaborative emphasis of SAP xApps and its ability to unify information across existing systems allow applications to support strategic processes that require a comprehensive view of the enterprise. This avoids time-consuming assembly and a rollup of information from component systems, records the decisions for later steps in the process, and manages group communication. All of this contributes to strategic efficiency, the essence of which is making decisions as fast as possible based on the right information.

---

1 Dan Woods: *Packaged Composite Applications: An O'Reilly Field Guide to Enterprise Software*. O'Reilly & Associates, Sebastopol 2003.

SAP xApps expands organizational awareness across departmental boundaries. While many versions of a specific enterprise application, such as human capital management (HCM), supplier relationship management (SRM), or customer relationship management (CRM), may exist in a company, each class of application is a world unto itself, separate from other classes. CRM and HCM both have employee information, but the functions that each application performs and the information stored are often completely distinct. The job of the SAP business process platform is to integrate those core enterprise resource planning (ERP) components and provide a service layer that can be used by SAP xApps to spin a web across classes of applications and create a comprehensive model of information and functionality from each. These cross-functional processes can be the key to larger efficiencies or competitive advantages.

Developing composite applications extends the ERP platform and minimizes disruptions to business-critical functions, because it doesn't rely on alterations to core application business logic or data structures. Businesses depend on the continued operation of their core ERP processes, often supported by legacy systems. Changes can introduce bugs that make doing business impossible, and as systems become increasingly more complex, the cost of making the next change increases exponentially. Composite applications allow new functionality to be delivered without modifying hard-to-change base systems. Once this new functionality has been established, it can be integrated into the core platform once again to become an additional service for other applications.

User-Centered Design

The second key concept behind developing composite applications is *user-centered design*—the discipline of specifying a new system based on an in-depth understanding of the detailed work practice of its users. Composite applications are cross-functional, highly interactive systems—far more complex than traditional forms-driven interfaces supporting database transactions—and are far more enmeshed in the day-to-day work of their users. Successful deployment of these systems cannot happen by management declaring that a new system must be employed by users—users have been working around systems that don't work well for them for years.

Management defines the project and states what's required. "Reduce travel costs," or "Meet the new environmental reporting regulations." If the system doesn't deliver on these expectations, it is a failure.

But it's the users of the system who determine whether or not the system will actually work. People organize their work to make their tasks efficient; they have intents (i.e., goals) that they are trying to achieve; they use strategies to achieve these intents and accomplish these tasks. Some of these tasks, intents, and strategies are explicitly defined; others are implicit and grow out of experience from doing the work. When looked at collectively, these tasks, intents, and strategies constitute the users' *work practice*. If the system supports and extends the work practice, it will be accepted; otherwise, users will subvert it. With the best of intentions, users will circumvent the system because they *must* get the job done somehow. "I know policy is to go through purchasing," one user might say. "But their vendor is more expensive—I'm just putting this purchase on our credit card." Or, "I'll do the bookkeeping work required by the system, but my *real* records are here in my trusty spreadsheet."

Understanding who the users are, how they work, and what their issues are is critical to meet the expectations of a project (not forgetting that we have to worry about all the users—including indirect users such as managers who depend on reports from the system and all the stakeholders who can affect its success.) We do this by adapting techniques from Contextual Design, the industry-leading process developed by Karen Holtzblatt and Hugh Beyer. Their book[2] describes the full Contextual Design process—here, we'll introduce a simplified and stream-

---

2 Hugh Beyer and Karen Holtzblatt: *Contextual Design: Defining Customer-Centered Systems.* Morgan Kaufmann Publishers, Inc., San Francisco 1997. For more information about CD and InContext services, go to *www.incontextdesign.com*.

lined design process tailored to the design of composite applications that addresses a business pain point within an enterprise.

Applying user-centered design to the development of composite applications starts by considering the *project scope*—the extent of change envisioned by a new project. Some projects envision fundamental change to the business practice; others seek only to streamline or simplify the way in which business is done. Composite applications can run the gamut from simple, fast-turnaround projects to fundamental business restructuring that may go so far as to redefine the relationships between businesses.

When analyzing project scope, we start by looking at the underlying *intent* of the business practice that the composite application will address. The intent is the goal or ultimate purpose of the practice, whether explicitly stated or entirely implicit. Some process intents include:

▶ *Creating customer value* in manufacturing or product creation

▶ *Making that value known* to customers in marketing and sales

▶ *Conforming to a set of externally imposed standards* like U.S. Food and Drug Administration (FDA) regulations, environmental compliance, or Global Trade Security

▶ *Providing an employee service* in human resources and benefits

▶ *Running the business itself* with accounting and financial tracking

▶ Redesigning business processes requires an understanding of such high-level business intents. The starting point for improving business processes is a clear and unambiguous description of the "as-is" practice—the way the business *currently* accomplishes the work. Such a concrete representation supports conversations about changes by getting everyone on the same page from the start.

Individual user data always plays an integral role in understanding the intent of the business process and the as-is practice. Process innovation requires that an organization is capable of seeing its own real-work practice. Once the practice has been revealed, it can be supported, extended, transformed, rationalized, or fixed to meet the requirements of the business.

A composite application also supports people's work tasks in a day-to-day, minute-by-minute fashion. The project stakeholders may have an abstract, high-level view of the work of a business process as it flows through their part of the organization, but this abstraction idealizes what really goes on in the daily life of the organization. Too much of what really happens in daily life is tacit; workers act in the context of their culture, using formal and informal procedures that have become habitual, responding to the usual and unusual daily tasks, through ongoing collaborations that make up the fabric of working life. These habits, expectations, and implicit rules of practice are no longer conscious. Traditional interviews with stakeholders are simply not the best source of information about the real business practice and they do not lead to the detailed data that interaction designers need.

For example, in the product innovation process, the formal process descriptions described a clean stage/gate handover process that ensures the standardization and quality of new product development. But it did not describe how individual product managers struggled to collect and consolidate new product ideas, represent the requirements clearly, and prioritize new features so that all would agree to the final product definition.

So to redesign the business process with attention to how things really work in practice, look at the day-to-day activities of real people and work groups. To understand the actual work practice of people, gather low-level detail about daily work life. The Contextual Design process reveals such work practice by observing real people doing the real jobs that keep their companies running.

Revealing the work practice of individuals as it is actually done requires two things:

▶ **Contextual Interviews**
Collecting observational data about what people really do by watching people work and talking with people in the context of their daily

life. Such field data is collected from all the key roles that make a process work. This data reveals what is really going on across the organization.

▶ **Work Modeling**
Techniques that lay out the original field data in the form of diagrams or other notations to represent the structure of the work, replete with all the variation of the real business. These models show the high-level business process as it really is with all the actual breakdowns and opportunities to guide redesign. They also show the low-level detail about roles and tasks that allow for design at the lower levels.

Spectacular failures have resulted from enterprise system implementations that failed to respect the work practice nuances and business model variations of the implementing organization. The key to successful requirements definition is to build detailed work models from reliable field data. The models articulate what people are doing, why they are doing it, and how the activities of one set of people impacts and drives the activities of others. This high-level picture of the as-is business process gives designers the tools to see what needs to be changed or improved. The detailed data embedded in the work models can be used to re-engineer work practice and to help the designer create a new system solution, define the concrete functionality, and pick the *UI building blocks* to use.

Development with UI Building Blocks

The third key concept of creating composite applications is development with UI building blocks: a set of platform components that can easily be assembled into a coherent system. These components help to synthesize user interface, workflow, and underlying information flow into a system design that is simple, effective, and intuitive for users.

UI building blocks are similar to using design patterns, which have become a popular theme in software development. Few problems are wholly new; in every area of design, we see the same patterns appear over and over again. In the design of enterprise systems, a few patterns of work practice repeat frequently. People organize their action items into task lists; they create triggers as reminders to do work; they follow step-by-step procedures to perform complex actions; and they monitor the state of the work that is under their control.

It's a waste of time and development resources to address these problems time and again, as though they were new. It's far better to design a powerful, effective solution for each work pattern only once and then, reuse this solution when needed. This is what the UI building blocks are, namely, an encapsulated software solution supporting a work practice pattern. Designed and tested with user-centered methods, they build effective user interface design and application flow into the system that incorporates them.

Projects based on UI building blocks focus on the business problem they are solving rather than on the details of UI design. Many development teams do not have the deep UI design skill required to design a good interface; even those that do rarely have the time in their project schedule to do more than barebones UI design. With all the other tasks of system design—structuring the data, designing workflows, figuring out how back-end connectivity should work—UI design tends to take a back seat. The UI building blocks help development teams create a system with a productive and pleasing user experience quickly.

We'll now introduce some of the key UI building blocks provided by the SAP business process platform, each of them supporting common work patterns:

▶ The *Control Center* provides a set of organizing views with an overview of the user's entire work history on a particular project. It collects work-related information into a set of distinct views, enabling the user to see what is urgent, track what is ongoing, and take action when necessary.

▶ *Work Centers* provide a single coherent place to do a set of closely related tasks. They collect the things being worked on, the views and status indicators for managing ongoing activities and receiving new work triggers, and the tools required to take action.

▶ *Ad-hoc Activity Centers* provide a coherent place to do ad-hoc work on a specific task or project. They collect the views and status indicators to monitor the ongoing activity, as well as everything else required to accomplish the task. They save the user's context for the duration of the task, and ensure that it disappears when it is no longer needed.

▶ *Guided Procedures* support business processes that may cross people or organizations. They give an overview of the entire process, including who the contributors are and the current state of the process; they also give individual contributors activity centers in which to do their part of the work.

▶ *Object instance views* provide workspaces for manipulating the objects representing business concerns (a customer order, for example). They allow state and properties of the object to be viewed and modified (as appropriate) and provide access to functions that work on that object.

▶ *Dashboards* provide at-a-glance information about ongoing work and business objects that are important to the user at a particular moment. They summarize the status, show key information, and provide access to the object or work process itself.

▶ *Worklists* display the list of work items that the user is asked to act upon. These work items can be pushed ad-hoc requests, system-generated business objects that require attention, or standard tasks generated by workflow for which the user is responsible.

By taking advantage of these building blocks, a development team eliminates much of its design work. The building blocks provide a user interface framework along with key elements of that user interface; they offer developers with a common method of accessing and presenting legacy data; and they make available a structure and models into which any new user interfaces can be designed.

Assembling a Composite Application

When building a composite application, the technology platform does the job of understanding and managing the internal connections. The designer starts with a set of abstractions for the user interface, core services provided by platform components like content management systems, and enterprise services for functionality provided by existing engines or applications. With these at hand, design becomes a straightforward process of mapping requirements to preexisting UI components.

In order to be effective, such a pattern-based design approach depends on having detailed data about the real work practice of the people in the organization. Without such data, the designer cannot respond to the real problems in the work and requirements cannot be mapped to UI building blocks that support a seamless work practice for their users.

This book will help you to understand how to collect and model requirements in such a way that they can be smoothly mapped to reusable UI building blocks such as those provided by SAP NetWeaver. With this understanding of the work practice, supported by the SAP business process platform and the reliable design patterns in the UI building blocks, businesses can start innovating again. The bar for the support of new ideas is lower. The time to market is shorter, which means more ideas can be implemented and more ideas will have a positive return on investment (ROI). Furthermore, the existing infrastructure can be leveraged to provide more information and functionality to a greater number of users.

The following is an example of an SAP xApps packaged composite application that was defined using SAP NetWeaver to solve real-world needs. Throughout the book, we'll return to this subject, that is, the composite application, to illustrate various points.

SAP xApp Product Definition (SAP xPD) addresses the needs of concept development and requirements management in the product lifecycle management (PLM) domain. The project team was chartered to find a business case for an application in the PLM domain, a key SAP business solution area and target software market. It was clear from the beginning that elements of traditional PLM—planning (such as product planning and implementation), design (such as computer-aided design tools), after-market provisioning (such as spare parts and service fleet management), and so on—were fairly mature market segments. However, the initial activities of the product lifecycle—things like idea capture, breaking down requirements, developing and evaluating a new concept, technical feasibility, and risk analysis—appear to have been largely ignored by other PLM software vendors.

Using a customer-centered design process similar to what we describe in this book, the SAP xPD development team produced an application for this area. It provides simple structures for surfacing and managing new requirements and product concepts, evaluating them through procedures that cut across multiple disciplines, and helping them to evolve into formal product proposals. The SAP xPD xApp coordinates the work of marketing research, business development, and product engineering to ensure that all perspectives contribute to the product concept. It provides summary management views of the number of product concepts under consideration and the state of those concepts. And it incorporates data from legacy systems without restructuring or re-implementing those systems.

We use the SAP xPD project as an example of the recommended design process throughout this book.

1   From Best Practice to Next Practice

Real work in companies is done by individuals working in the context of a larger business process. Traditional application development paradigms focus almost exclusively on the business process, without much consideration for the design of the individual work practice that actually gets the work done. With composite applications, you can design business process and user work practice together to better achieve business goals, reduce business operational expenses, and, perhaps most importantly, introduce process innovations that increase business opportunities.

Business process and work practice innovations come from exploiting corporate core competencies, capitalizing on disruptive events and technologies, and building in industry knowledge. We're talking about looking beyond *best practice*—the best of what industry is doing now. We want to invent *next practices*—new, better practices introducing new processes that enable new work practice and transform organizational roles—and possibly transform the entire company culture.

In this chapter, we substantiate these claims. We look at how development drives innovation from the perspectives of process—the defined business structure and procedures; from work practice—what people actually do on a daily basis; and from change impact—how we introduce changes into an already functioning business.

1.1   Composite Applications Drive Innovation

Businesses must deliver revenue-generating products and services that meet market needs and are produced efficiently. The job of a manager, as business management guru W. Edwards Deming[1] says, is to ensure efficiency, stability, and predictability in the processes of the company. Well-managed processes enable an organization to focus on creating value through new product and service offerings, because workers can

---

1 W. Edwards Deming: *Out of Crisis*. Massachusetts Institute of Technology Center for Advanced Engineering Study, 1982.

focus on *what* they are doing, not *how* they are doing it. So, for a business, innovation must create new and transformative processes that help businesses get their work done better.

We can do this by creating composite applications that sit on top of services from many underlying systems. These applications have a greater degree of freedom to optimize the user experience and provide new tools for supporting and extending the way in which people work. For example, they may include integrated analytics, collaborative services, and dynamic workflows to provide the context for a task.

Combining those technological advances with good design practices refocuses the development project on the "what" of a business process. It also opens up the design scope beyond just the business process. Furthermore, it takes into consideration work group support and people productivity.

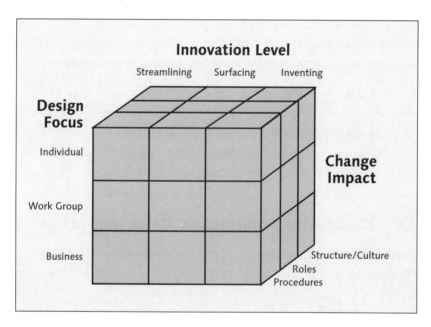

Figure 1.1 Dimensions of Innovation Introduced by Composite Applications

The innovation cube shown in Figure 1.1 introduces three major dimensions, along which composite applications drive innovation or impact the way we run the business.

In the following sections, we will discuss each dimension of innovation and the role of customer data in supporting such innovation. Then, in the following chapters, we'll show you how to implement these ideas in actual projects.

1.2 Innovation Level

We define three levels of process innovation that range from near-term, simple improvements to the day-to-day work of people in the company, to invention and implementation of wholly new ways of doing business. Depending on the business need and level of commitment, composite applications can support innovation at any level. We call these levels *streamlining*, *surfacing*, and *inventing*.

1.2.1 Streamlining Existing Processes

Often the problem facing an organization isn't that a process is fundamentally wrong—it's that the work required to do the process is so cumbersome that productivity is seriously degraded. *Streamlining* the existing process innovates by discovering and fixing the real productivity problems that are obstacles for people getting the work done.

In these cases, a defined business practice already exists. Manufacturing line processes, for example, could not exist without a defined method. Even in "softer" areas of the business—such as travel and reimbursement—policies and procedures are defined. They are intended to support an efficient way of meeting business goals, conforming to legal requirements, and ensuring appropriate communication and documentation.

Composite applications *streamline* existing business practices by fixing breakdowns and introducing changes, such as system automation, to increase process efficiency and effectiveness. Where the practice is broken or poorly integrated (when viewed from the perspective of the whole business), a streamlining composite application improves the system support for the process. In these cases, work practice doesn't suffer from a lack of formalization. System support for the targeted process may exist but is incomplete or is lacking adequate system integration. Streamlining applications target the inadequate nature of this support for redesign.

Composite applications, by design, cut across and integrate data from multiple business systems. They use collaborative technology to bring together the people who need to coordinate to get the work done. They raise information up from where it is hidden in a department's systems and provide the right level of detail for the worker and the manager alike. And they introduce organized workflow, supporting the everyday activities of the people carrying out the work.

Field data is critical to such an endeavor. First, designers need to know where the process has problems, performance inefficiencies, and informal workarounds so that these issues can become the subject of the design effort. Secondly, no single user or business function has a clear view of the whole process. A thorough understanding of all aspects of the work practice is required to develop an application that ties everything together. The result is the same basic process as before, but streamlined and improved.

1.2.2 Surfacing Hidden Processes

Some processes are poorly supported simply because no one in the business has thought to take them seriously as processes. People make their work by inventing ad-hoc ways to get things done. Over time, these inventions become the standard way to do things, without anyone ever planning them or thinking through how they support the goals of the enterprise.

Some processes are clearly core to the business and get management's attention from the beginning. Manufacturing is explicitly modeled, defined, and continuously refined. But consider processes like product-concept generation or software design. These are also critical to business success, but the work process is implicit and its structure is unexamined. A bird's-eye view of these processes looks like people talking by the coffee machine, having weekly coordination meetings, creating project plans, and chatting about what they are doing or creating.

Managers tend to think of managing these processes in terms of communication, coordination, team dynamics, and documentation of the designs and decisions. The process as a process is not explicitly defined.

New technologies can create new hidden processes that tend to grow up around these technologies without explicit design or support. web publishing is one example. A company decides to have a web page and then people start to push information they want to make available on the web to the webmaster. Slowly, informal procedures are developed for deciding on a new section of the website, finding and creating the right materials, and reviewing changes. But these processes occur in email, in face-to-face meetings, in phone conversations, and by individuals running around trying to get buy-in from the involved parties. Companies are now realizing that they must manage these processes like a real production process if they are going to improve the efficiency of their organization and leverage reuse of time and materials.

Companies can gain a huge business advantage by recognizing hidden processes, raising them up to awareness, and designing for them explicitly. Good application design makes hidden processes explicit by providing support for teams and work group practice; formalizing and documenting decisions, and making tacit work explicit and manageable. Whenever a business can start to see, plan for, and manage undefined processes that are core to the business, real business transformation becomes possible. Invisible processes are transformed into managed processes.

But putting a new system in place depends on understanding the implicit process—the activities, goals, and actions that the business has come to depend on without any explicit design. Field data becomes critical for understanding what the needs are and for recognizing all the inefficiencies in the existing way of doing things. Based on this data, process redesign that introduces technology sensibly can refocus the enterprise on creating business value. Consequently, hidden processes in an organization will be uncovered so they can be understood, improved, and used to inform the design of enterprise systems.

1.2.3 Inventing Processes

But what about creating new processes? *Inventing* business processes is the third level of innovation. As new technologies and new approaches to businesses evolve, they create the opportunity to structure business processes in fundamentally new ways. But, because these are new approaches to business, they cannot follow existing state-of-the-art or best practices. Instead, they must come directly from understanding the work practice, the technology, and the business.

Sometimes the driver for invention comes from the outside. For example, the new wastewater-management regulations in the European Union made it necessary for all manufacturing companies to respond with manufacturing-line changes and changes to internal procedures so they could file the necessary reports. Or look at the way the success of web technology has created new marketing opportunities for forward-looking companies. Dell took advantage of this opportunity and created an entirely new customer relationship with its "Dell Direct" sales model. In each case, changes in the external business climate drove internal change.

The driver for invention can also be internal. Internal change may come from a desire to make existing practices more efficient or may result in a change in focus—a change in what the business includes within its management purview. Over the last 10 years, the major auto manufacturers decided that they were spending too much time and using too many resources, working with hundreds of suppliers and subcontractors. They lobbied to work with only a few large subcontractors and, consequently, restructured the auto business by requiring all subcontractors to integrate their manufacturing and inventory management across business boundaries. The internal process changes needed to tie the subcontractors into the business required process invention at all levels.

A service-oriented development platform such as SAP NetWeaver can help businesses rise to these internal and external challenges. Because the platform allows development across business boundaries, connecting people, data, and existing applications, innovation does not have to mean throwing out all the old systems and starting from scratch. More-over, because such platforms enable composite applications to support collaboration and information sharing, they can bring cross- and within-business work groups together around new defined procedures.

But data about how people and businesses work is needed to reveal their intents—what they are trying to accomplish in the work as it is currently structured. Modeling the current work practice provides the lens necessary to really see what is going on, before trying to achieve those intents in a new way. With this understanding, it becomes possi-ble to reinvent safely—to introduce new procedures knowing that they will serve the needs of the business. It is risky for a personal computer vendor to completely change its sales channel, or for a manufacturer to completely revamp its supplier relationship. Having detailed data about how the business works drives process invention and reduces the risk.

1.3   Design Focus

Our next dimension is the design focus. The term "business process reengineering" tends to hide the fact that the success and efficiency of all business process is the result of what *people* do. Even fully auto-mated environments that depend on robots and complex machines need people to feed, monitor, and fix those machines. Therefore, it is the entire work practice around a formally defined business process that matters for application design.

1.3.1   Designing Beyond Business Processes

When redesigning work practice, there are three levels to consider: the *business process* and its associated business rules and workflow; the *work group* that operates to achieve a particular goal at different points in the process; and the *individual* who carries out and organizes daily work within the context of the work group and larger business process. To keep the business running on a heterogeneous system landscape, we need to empower people to make decisions and connect them to the processes that are made up of the tasks they perform.

A composite application will be successful only if all three levels are designed together to ensure value to the business, the work group, and the individual. People make the processes work, so value must be delivered to individuals or they will not operate within the new business process willingly. Instead, people will circumvent the formal process to get the real work of the business done—creating yet another undefined business practice that becomes hard to track and manage.

Consider the model of the manufacturing line. Not only do line designers have to plan how product and raw materials move from station to station, they must also define how the people at each station will work individually and together. If the designers focus only on workflow definition and business process definition without looking at how work groups organize themselves and coordinate with others, they will miss significant innovation and efficiency improvements. If designers focus only on how individuals fit into a process or work group without looking at increasing productivity on the desktop, they will miss the opportunity to optimize work organization. Or worse, they will overlook what business process redesign does to individual and group practice and introduce inefficiency and breakdowns along with the introduction of new technologies.

Work practice analysis breaks down the larger black boxes of the business process and looks at the detailed steps that the group and the individual take to get the work done. Sharpening the focus of process design from the overall business process to the individual work practice depends on discovering the details of people's work practice. One can only design for what one knows—if designers only know how to look at business process, they can design only business process. If they know how individual work practice is structured and how work groups cooperate and coordinate their work, they can innovate at this level also. For that reason, field data is the prerequisite for work practice innovation.

1.3.2 Work Group Collaboration

No one works alone. People in businesses are always part of a work group, often multiple overlapping work groups, which implicitly or explicitly are part of a larger business process. These teams, formal and informal, communicate and collaborate to get the work done. Work groups share information, designs, and project status. They review each other's work, create and change schedules, approve requests, pass tasks, and create events. Work groups may be colocated, but frequently are widely distributed. Rarely do work groups have a physical place to continuously work together. They rely on technologies like email, shared data stores, phone, and fax to make their collaboration work.

Work groups rarely have tools that make collaboration and information sharing easy; far too much is hidden in separate data stores and in myriad places on an intranet. Technology has created a sea of information, overwhelming the individual teams who are expected to publish, find, use, and update public information as an additional part of their worker role.

Moreover, formal teams tasked with producing a product rarely think about how they participate in the implicit management work group created by the management hierarchy. Executive management, general managers, and directors see the teams in their organizations as part of their larger work group. Managers depend on the visibility of what their teams are doing to ensure the success of the business strategy.

The framework of the SAP NetWeaver platform provides building blocks and related services to integrate information directly into the business context. For example, Guided Procedures can help to share all resources of one process and coordinate all actors of that process. Composite applications like SAP xApp Product Definition (SAP xPD) use this building block to track the development of product concepts.

Business systems tend to ignore the needs of the management work group. Managers do not have information to answer their questions about their campaigns, strategies, and business process status. Nor can they easily coordinate and collaborate vertically to get this visibility. Even horizontally—working with other management teams—the management work group is hampered by the challenge of communication, coordination, and tracking. Redesigning work group practice looks beyond the needs of a single person and examines how people work together in an abstract high-level business process. It designs for how people might work within a collaborative network that accomplishes tasks and tracks business goals together.

Take the production supervisor as an example. One standard collaborative scenario is the daily communication and coordination with colleagues on other shifts, ensuring that everyone has the same context across shifts. Supporting the work group requires supporting all key players related to a business process, whether they are an actor within the process or an overseer of it, and whether they are involved in a single process or many.

Seeing the as-is practice to streamline it, reveal it, and invent something new requires knowing *who* to look at. Collecting field data reveals work practice, if it is collected from the key players in the business process. These include the formal groups found in organization charts and project plans as well as the informal groups that come together to solve specific problems—the management structure responsible for overseeing the work, as well as the horizontal network of peers working together. Recognizing and analyzing these collaborations creates opportunities for innovation.

Composite applications are capable of bringing together information, providing status, creating contexts for productive coordination and communication, and moving tasks and information between work group members. Innovation results from designing *how* the people in the work groups will work so that they can focus on *what* that work group is to accomplish.

1.3.3   Individual User Productivity

Individuals participate in work groups and are part of the larger business process. To do this, they have to accomplish their individual tasks and organize their personal work. If the individual's work is not efficient, coordinated with their work group, and supportive of the business goal, innovation at any other level cannot be realized.

People must organize their incoming work and fulfill outstanding requests. They must find information, pass information, create products, perform services, attend meetings, return phone calls, fill out forms, and do all the tasks that are expected of them. To do this, they are given multiple nonintegrated systems that do not combine data as needed, so people become the data integrators. People feel that they work with seemingly arbitrary procedures, lacking clear goals or measures of progress, that are so cumbersome they hinder the work rather than help it. People have to do some of their work on paper and some online. They find the old ways of working before automation simpler than the new ways employing unreliable technology. Even the simple business of organizing oneself becomes overwhelming when so much is communicated by phone, fax, email, and "drop-ins."

Just improving work practice at the level of the individual can increase efficiency of the overall work group and business process. If a business-process redesign project sees individuals' work only as a source of data, individual work can become mindless data entry. If individual work is seen as a step at the end of a defined workflow, with no consideration for the collaboration that occurs at that step, work group activities will not be supported. And if optimizing the work is seen as fixing a single task, system, or process problem, the productivity of workers will be reduced, because the coherence of their work will be fragmented.

Good process redesign must increase productivity at the level of the individual, supporting the whole work process by providing the information, task tracking, tools, procedure guidance, and access to collaboration that individuals need to get work done. Individual work practice can be optimized only if the work role, the related work intent, information needs, and collaboration needs are understood. Field data that reveals the needs of the individual can allow designers to step back and redesign the work of the individual within the context of the work group and the business process. Field data reveals the roles and activities of employees necessary for driving the design of individual Work Centers, so that everything needed by the individual is readily available.

Understanding the work of the individual as the basis for process design has an immediate benefit for the business. For example, dashboards acting as watch lists of important business activities bring the information needed to monitor ongoing processes to the user's desktop. The user is made aware of status changes and is able to react to new business situations. This and other building blocks ensure that users can find the information they need, share information in the context of work, and educate themselves to run their processes more efficiently. The resulting streamlining of individual work practice shows up as increased productivity, with fewer errors, and quicker results.

Composite applications—with their focus on connecting the individual to business processes based on roles, activities, and collaborations— can contribute significantly and quickly to increased user productivity.

Effective innovation reaches deep into the daily lives of the people in an organization. It is not enough to optimize business process flow from person to person, department to department, or company to company. Real innovation comes at the desktop, where real people do their tasks, manage their priorities, and oversee business processes. Composite applications, when designed with field data, can create business value at all three levels of practice.

1.4   Impact of Change

Innovation means change: change regarding how individuals work, how groups work together, how business goals are achieved, and, ultimately, change to the overall business culture. An organization's ability to manage change determines whether innovation can succeed. If new technology makes achieving that organization's intent more difficult, people will ignore it or work around it. For innovation to be successful, designers must keep in mind the actual impact of the change and plan accordingly for it.

Innovative software applications have the potential to change work in two ways: by making operational changes in the organization and by introducing technology. Change management, indeed risk mitigation, is as much related to how innovation is introduced as to the design itself. Depending on the design of the application and its innovation level (streamlining, surfacing, or inventing), software can introduce minor or significant changes as to how people work. Depending on the quality of the user experience, adopting a new system can be easy or irritating. But driving process change and system design from field data and then refining the design with the future users ensures high-quality work-practice redesign and user experience. A user-centered design process keeps the focus on how the redesign will impact people's lives. This is the best assurance of effective change management.

1.4.1 Changes in Procedures

Procedures at the level of the individual and work group tend to be tacit and ad hoc. Procedures to get individual work done are passed on informally from experienced workers to new colleagues. Procedures for how to run groups are not articulated. Procedures for how to do the tasks defined by business processes are not well defined. Yet all the work of the business comes down to procedures at this level.

Individuals, groups, and process definers may create paper checklists of what to do for given tasks. These lists may be individual or shared. They may be formal methods for doing the work, or they may capture informal learning over time. Rarely does large-scale process redesign address these task-oriented procedures. When system design does not reveal and support these activities, its very limitations may inadvertently complicate the work and decrease productivity.

Composite applications like Guided Procedures can reveal task procedures, attach appropriate information to each step, call up relevant application components, allow people to record what is done and what is not, and move task information between people in a workflow while retaining context and history. Revealing and defining procedures helps new people learn how to do the work and ensures that experienced people can accomplish the steps without skipping a step, losing information, or duplicating effort through redundant data entry.

Not only applications that invent new processes, but also applications that streamline and surface processes lead to adaptations of the work procedures. Users will perform their existing procedures more efficiently due to new levels of data and process integration. Procedures that served only as workarounds due to system design limitations will disappear.

1.4.2 Changes in Roles and Responsibilities

Any process redesign changes people's roles and responsibilities. Shifting tasks from one knowledge worker to another with a different set of skills changes expectations of people and departments. Bringing information together to support each person's entire body of work changes collaboration, teamwork, and management interaction, as well as the extent of administrative help that a person might need. All this disrupts people's lives.

Composite applications streamline work practice by simplifying difficult tasks, making information more easily accessible, and supporting changes in personnel by shifting a coherent set of responsibilities from one person to another in a simple step. Entire work roles may be automated; new roles may be introduced. Revealed processes may now have managers overseeing them. Process changes may introduce role changes. New system features may introduce the need for system or information support.

To create and plan for change in the organization means changing people's roles and behaviors at the level of their individual work, how they collaborate and coordinate with others, and how they participate in a larger department or business process. Change is always hard to design right, and to win people's acceptance. Gathering user data reveals the waste in the current processes driving change to how people work. Refining the organizational and system design with users' involvement lets them participate in co-designing future roles and systems, thereby increasing the probability of future buy-in. This transparency ensures that people know the value of the changes—what's in it for them—so they can accept new practices more readily. Resistance to change is managed through the user-centered redesign process.

1.4.3 Changes in Structure and Culture

Invariably, changes in business processes, work practices, and systems cause cultural change within the business. If the cultural change supports business goals and human values, the business will adopt the new practices. But, if system changes devalue the individual or undermine business goals, people will resist the new system. Balancing the conflict between the goals of the business and the value of the person is a major challenge in system design.

For example, enhanced business intelligence systems bring information together coherently so that business information collected downstream—on the manufacturing floor or from the sales force—is available to managers via upstream steps in a business process. Central data warehouse applications often ask field people to enter data into the system in addition to their normal tasks. This makes it possible to give aggregated key performance indicators (KPIs) to management immediately. This "zero-latency" information enables management to respond quickly—a closed-loop process that efficiently manages a dynamically changing business.

However, if employees are forced to enter data without receiving any personal benefit, they will view this as an onerous, time-wasting chore and resist doing it. Creating a policy to enforce data entry does not eliminate the resistance; it just disempowers employees and creates resentment.

Designers who take cultural changes into consideration can avoid this problem. Good system design is mindful of the impact of change on everyone involved. Good designers are careful not to undermine positive aspects of corporate culture. Moving data entry back in the process to where the data was created is one way to eliminate mindless work, thereby releasing employees to use their knowledge instead. Such a change creates a valuing culture that itself fosters the desire to contribute.

Similarly, introducing new technologies can conflict with corporate or country culture. Accessibility to skill evaluations, personal data about employees, and transparent tracking and measuring of task completion can provide information to aid management. But in some countries, these same features are seen as invasions of privacy. Redesign always occurs within the culture of the country and the company. As such, good redesign must consider explicit and implicit changes to culture in order to ensure that adoption is successful.

1.5   Feeding Innovation

To summarize, innovation needs:

▶ A way to collect and model user data about existing practice that produces a reliable reflection of practice at every level

▶ A business process platform that can implement the redesigned work

▶ A system redesign process that involves work groups and users in co-designing the change to ensure its quality and to manage its adoption

▶ Designers who have the skills in the technology, in customer-centered design techniques, and in the business to develop and implement these redesigns

▶ Organizations that desire change and have processes for managing their impact

Composite applications allow companies to build, support, and monitor processes in ways that were not possible previously. The potential value to the corporation is enormous. But the effectiveness of the application, in the long run, is only as good as the human process that it puts in place. Design from user data helps to ensure that applications support the business, the work group and the individual. User-centered design, by definition, puts cultural impact and issues of user adoption at the center of the design process. The design process as described in this book is a healthy marriage between the power of technology and the needs of the people it is meant to support.

In the next chapter, we turn our attention to evaluating the potential of a composite application development project and discuss how to effectively scope out the opportunity domain and the design project itself.

2   Problem Analysis

Whether reinventing a business process or supporting a work process or existing practice better, the first task of any design group is to understand the nature and the scope of the problem. So we'll start our discussion by looking at how to approach the problem itself. Development of composite application on top of a service-oriented technology platform is a powerful way to create enterprise applications. But is it the right tool for every problem your business faces? Certain aspects of a problem suggest composite application development as the most effective approach: if requirements cross traditional business functions; if customizing off-the-shelf solutions has high risk; if you face highly collaborative group workflows; and, if you are designing next practice that is beyond the standard. These features can call for the development of a composite application, but even then, the problem must be scoped and a development approach must be chosen.

Remember that our recommended design process builds on the Contextual Design (CD) user-centered process and the UI building blocks. This powerful combination of process and technology enables rapid development of composite applications. The UI building blocks, themselves developed with CD techniques, incorporate work practice innovations that are useful across a wide variety of business practices. Building on these innovations reduces the amount of detailed customer data that a design team needs. When building blocks are appropriate for supporting the work, design is reduced to collecting the data required to instantiate the building blocks appropriate to that business process area. Only when no building block exists is it necessary to get detailed work-practice data and design wholly new interfaces.

To further simplify the development of composite applications, we will introduce *project structures* organized around the innovation dimension of the innovation cube introduced earlier—streamlining, surfacing, and inventing. Each level of process innovation implies the existence of a particular project structure that gathers customer data appropriate to the business problem, models the business at the necessary level, and iterates solutions incorporating the UI building blocks provided by SAP NetWeaver.

But before taking advantage of this approach, the project team must orient itself to the problem. That means the following: first, scoping the project; second, choosing the right project structure; and third, if necessary, building an initial prototype.

2.1 Scoping the Project

The first step to building a business solution is to analyze the problem and determine how to approach it. At this point, you may want to investigate industry practice in general and your market in particular to understand the state of the art for the problem. Teams developing applications for internal use also look at general industry practice for benchmarking purposes. Discussions with marketing or the affected management team help clarify the problem. Through these activities, the entire team comes to understand the nature of the problem.

The next step is to consider how to structure the project. This decision is driven by the nature of the project. You have to decide on the type of innovation project and the kind of field data needed to support it. At this time, you should raise questions such as:

▶ **Who are the direct users of the proposed application?**
What roles do they play in their organization? What are the key tasks the application will support? Which work group do they belong to? Identifying the primary users allows you to focus on the business, tasks, and collaboration that are affected by the project. In product innovation, management target roles are, for example, the product managers, the various product stakeholders like technology experts and marketing people, and the constraint setters like packaging, legal, and manufacturing.

▶ **Is there a defined workflow?**
Does the proposed application address work practice for which explicit procedures exist? A defined, understood workflow suggests a streamlining project—as long as the workflow really *is* well under-

stood and is actually done according to the formal definition. Sometimes a company has a defined workflow, but much of the work is still done outside of the formal process. In this case, you are going to both streamline and surface the process for better support and redesign. Product innovation management is a good example of a process that has some formal organizational expectations but also has many activities, particularly collaboration, which occurred outside this loosely defined process.

▶ **Do the work tasks already exist?**

When new business practice is being introduced—for example, data must be tracked and reported to meet federal requirements, or inventory on a retailer's shelf must be tracked and replenished automatically by its supplier—the work practice to be supported doesn't actually exist yet. This indicates an inventing project.

Sometimes management has already decided on a new business process to be implemented. The challenge here is to optimize the work and business process at the level of the work group and organization. In this case, you need to collect data on existing processes that will be superseded by the new process to ensure a complete transition of supported activities. If the process is really new to the company, looking at related workflows—for example other quality or compliance tracking processes regarding conformance with new regulations—would be helpful to ensure that the new process works for the people who will carry it out.

▶ **Do systems already support these tasks?**

If there are systems already in place for the key work tasks, this suggests a streamlining project. If the project will put in place formal systems for the first time, or if people often circumvent existing legacy systems, this indicates a surfacing project. For example, the SAP xPD project supported new concept development. There were no systems providing direct support for this work; it was managed entirely through Microsoft Office documents and email. In other cases, existing systems will have to be integrated into the new processes.

▶ **What collaboration does the job require?**

Do these job roles depend on a high degree of collaboration across traditional business divisions, or will the design support a coherent work group? Designing for a work group that crosses organizational boundaries increases complexity and suggests Guided Procedures as the UI building blocks, which organize work across people. For example, in the innovation management project, new product ideas have to be aligned with later aspects of the product life cycle, such as marketing experts responsible for product launch and regional experts responsible for localization.

▶ **What are the primary work objects?**

The objects manipulated in doing the work become the important elements to represent in the final design. Unless an existing work object is rendered irrelevant in the redesign, users will want to create, track, and pass around the work objects that represent the work. These objects will be important to the content of the UI. In product innovation management, some key work objects are the product idea describing the new product feature or the market need; the product concept substantiating this idea; and the formal requirements driving the product specifications.

▶ **What UI building blocks are applicable?**

Even before gathering the first round of user data, basic familiarity with the problem space enables designers to make a good guess at which building blocks a project is likely to use. The more building blocks a development team can reuse or modify to support the business process, the more focused the data collection and design can be.

These questions will guide you in understanding the basic structure of the work process that they are going to support. They will help to clarify whether the project should use a streamlining, surfacing, or inventing pattern. Furthermore, they will help you to begin to define the kind of customer data that may be required and the technology challenges that you might encounter.

SAP xPD Project Scope

▶ **Direct Users**
Marketing research analysts, marketing research managers, product managers, engineering, and operations manager

▶ **Work Tasks**
Generate and present new concepts, run consumer studies, run tests of new concepts, review and evaluate new concepts, and so on

▶ **Systems Support**
No formal support: word processing and email only

▶ **Collaboration**
Cross-functional—marketing, engineering, operations

▶ **Work Objects**
Product idea and concept, requirements, solutions, products, and product components

▶ **UI Building Blocks**
Guided Procedures, Activity Center, object instance views

2.2 Determining the Project Structure

The next step is to use the aforementioned analysis to determine which project variant is most appropriate. This is determined by the level of innovation required. This book introduces three project variants, each tailored to a particular level of innovation by suggesting a slightly different project structure. As you will see, each variant requires a different level of organizational commitment and a different amount of time.

2.2.1 Streamlining Projects

Projects that fall into the *streamlining* category can typically be executed quickly, because the need for requirements gathering is comparatively small. In most streamlining projects, you can understand existing processes reasonably well by looking at legacy systems and process documentation. Stakeholders can often articulate the key pain points and value proposition readily. Therefore, you can often afford to shorten the initial data gathering steps and move straight to UI design.

For example, a company may manage its new product ideas through a paper document process. But this process suffers because information in the documents is not integrated with information in the product life-cyle management (PLM) system that actually defines the product's current properties. Building a composite application that brings these two processes together, and that integrates processes and data of early and later product development, is a classic example of a streamlined project that enhances existing processes.

When working on a streamlining application that addresses workflows crossing organizational boundaries, we have found that both technical and organizational considerations become a central focus. On the technical front, it is important for most streamlining projects to determine which system will serve as the primary holder of key data objects. The problems of working across legacy systems must be solved. For example, if a group of transactions spanning multiple systems must either all succeed or all fail, where will coordination take place and how will compensating transactions be managed?

On the organizational front, internal projects must involve key business stakeholders early on in the project. This is important not only for setting up interviews with the right users, but also for considering issues of acceptance and application-workflow ownership. In some streamlining projects, business stakeholders might feel threatened and resist active participation in the project. These stakeholders may be concerned that their organization's role in the process will be diminished somehow by the new solution. Or users may be afraid that the application will do little more than complicate their lives and increase their workload. Bringing stakeholders and users into the process early on, and providing consistent, clear communication about the goals and the status of the project, can help to minimize the organizational risks that can jeopardize a streamlining project.

When developing a product for a market, you don't have an internal customer to please; instead, you must ensure that you meet the demands of a whole market. There is the opportunity to work with a selected range of representative users and customer organizations. SAP has been very successful in the joint development of a first xApp release with pilot customers. The relationship with pilot customers facilitates setting up field interviews and intensive discussions with stakeholders. Ideally, pilot customers should have similar processes already in place. This turns an SAP xApp project into a streamlining project; however, for other customers, the SAP xApp application may represent next practice.

All streamlining projects call for moving quickly to a prototype that can be tested with users. This is possible when an analysis of the business process to be streamlined indicates that much of the process can be supported by tailoring existing UI building blocks to improve the flow of work and productivity. By iterating this prototype, you can quickly develop a powerful and effective application that fits seamlessly into the users' work.

But if inefficiencies of the target process have spawned alternative ways of working that take place outside the existing system and organizational management structure, this streamlining project has turned into a surfacing project. In this case, additional data should be collected to understand the hidden aspects of the process. Then, you can augment the design patterns to ensure that the entire process is supported appropriately.

2.2.2 Surfacing Projects

Surfacing projects require additional data and deliberate design. The work practice to be addressed is undefined and ad hoc with work groups collaborating through informal methods. Legacy systems, if any, have not been designed with the whole practice in mind; the process is typically held together with standard office software tools.

In product innovation management, users are engaged in the process of collecting process ideas, yet the system that is to be supported is still not in place. Implementing a system allows both the definition and redesign of the process that evolved over time.

A surfacing project produces a system that explicitly supports the critical activities of highly collaborative workflows. Alternatively, it integrates related data that used to be distributed across several back-end systems, thereby creating a new view on the business—turning hidden information into explicit analytics. Like streamlining projects, the processes targeted by a surfacing project exist; however, they have more interpersonal work dependencies, less distinct workflows, and less explicit information shared by group members. Each participant is likely to have a unique story about what "really" goes on in the work, but is usually telling only one part of a larger story.

Relative to streamlining projects, surfacing projects address business value loss that is typically hidden, or otherwise difficult to quantify. You must ensure that you understand the informal workarounds people have put in place to make the existing work practice successful; only then can you be confident in introducing changes. The project structure we will give you for these projects ensures that current practice is understood and represented explicitly before designing system support.

Contrary to streamlining projects, surfacing projects require more time and resource investment during the initial requirements-gathering phase of the application design roadmap. Since it is unlikely that you will find documentation or system representations for existing collaborative or informal processes, you must rely more heavily on gathering field data from users to understand the real-work practice, recognize which tacit processes need system support, see where collaboration is broken, and determine precisely what are the information and communication needs of the target work group.

In Chapter 1, we described web publishing as an example of a process that is hidden in many businesses. This is a classic example of a surfacing project. Product managers consider the web as only one of several distribution channels and write marketing materials without targeting the web in particular. Engineers write technical material the same way. On the other side of the organization, a website content owner hunts for all these materials, converting them into HTML, and reworking their content for a web audience. Whether they realize it, the product manager, engineer, and web content owner are all participating in an extended collaborative work group not found on any organization chart.

Much of the work of the modern enterprise is naturally collaborative, though its collaborative nature is often not recognized. Such implicit work group processes make some of the best candidates for composite applications. Work groups can be supported by surfacing informal collaboration and making it explicit system-supported activity, if possible, through reuse of existing UI building blocks.

In some surfacing projects, you might find that power users of office applications have effectively built them into their own work practices and that of their work group's as well. This is particularly true with applications like Microsoft Excel. We have seen demand-planning organizations at large companies that have created informal consensus-forecasting processes using Excel macros and email attachments. The payoff for closely studying what works and what doesn't in such cases ensures that you design a new solution that provides the same value and flexibility (or more) but within a managed process.

When developing for a market, this technique of observing what users have created in practice is very powerful. Your design team has the unique opportunity of seeing a wide range of ad-hoc, informal process structures. You can see common problems and workarounds, identify natural ways of organizing the work, and incorporate unique solutions into the product you design.

2.2.3 Inventing Projects

Inventing projects introduces new business processes. These projects must ensure they meet the business goal and also work for the people in the organization—people who will be working in processes and workflows that do not currently exist. The challenge for such a project is to introduce a new work practice that provides business value and works for people *the first time*. It's just too expensive to introduce a broken process with inadequate support and then try to fix it later.

For example, in the product innovation area, you might invent a composite application that changes the concept of requirements gathering and therefore its management. You might introduce product communities that establish a continuous conversation between development and users about how to improve a product. This requires a new community process to manage the customers, roles to support this community, processes to determine what ideas are worth pursuing, and so forth. In this example, you are inventing a new way to do business. You are not just streamlining an existing process.

To ensure the success of these innovation projects, you collect field data and use a more extensive set of work models to characterize the needs of the players involved in this scenario. The work models enable the design team to see the structure of the work into which the invention will fit. For example, you could study existing customer feedback channels and user associations to learn what users want to articulate about a product. The work models can also be used to analyze similar work practice; for example, data collected from people in open-source communities where product improvements are suggested and implemented by communities already today.

Working closely with an external or internal pilot customer or two is especially valuable for inventing projects. Because the change to work practice is substantial and the impact of the change is hard to foresee, a pilot customer provides an environment for iterating the design solution. You can see how an organization experiences the change and makes adjustments before going to a full release.

Streamlining and surfacing projects support organizations by fixing what is there and broken, whether explicit and screaming for attention or tacit and silently losing business value. In these cases, the project is a response to something experienced internally by the business. The inventing project responds to new stimuli that is internal or external to the business. In many cases, entirely new processes and work roles are the result of this effort. Inventing projects benefit from a more robust user-centered design process to ensure that the new process achieves the business goals *and* supports the work of the people who carry out the new process.

Whether your problem is streamlining an existing business process, surfacing and redefining an informal process, inventing a new process, or, more likely some combination of them all, composite applications that are designed based on user data can help you meet your business goals faster.

2.3   Building the Proof-of-Concept Prototype

Simply having a new hot idea for an application is not enough, unless you have a business case for it. Management is not likely to commit to a project without a business case showing that it is worth doing. This requires investments in market research and field research to describe a realistic business scenario and to identify the project's value proposition. This is the paradox of systems development. Management needs to know what a project will deliver before committing to it; but, until the project has gathered and analyzed requirements, it cannot be specific about what it will deliver.

This business case strengthens the team's own understanding of the problem and the approach they will use to solve it. For a product, such a business case should include an analysis of the market and competitors, the business need, and potential benefit.

As part of this work, it is often useful to develop an initial fast-turnaround prototype. This prototype allows the design team to explore the possible solution space; it demonstrates potential benefit to project stakeholders; and it can generate interest and excitement among external customers or internal users. The use of UI building blocks can be helpful in producing quick prototypes to give management a flavor for possible solutions.

Since resources are limited at this point, the team needs to collect as much information about the design space as possible, as quickly and cheaply as possible. A literature review reveals the current state of the art in the domain of interest, including techniques for managing the business process itself.

Informal interviews with internal stakeholders should also be conducted. Marketing and field service can easily be interviewed if the design is for a product. Internal projects should also include interviews with managers and other stakeholders in the new process.

If you decide to build an initial prototype for a product or an internal design, some field interviews should be conducted with potential end users. Field interviews are one-on-one, one-to-two-hour sessions conducted in users' workplaces. Keep the number of interviews and logistics costs low—there's no management buy-in yet, and probably no budget in place to support a larger effort.

If you're selling to a market, have patience with sales people who may not want the interviewing process to get in the way of important customer relationships. In this case, coupling field interviews with a prearranged meeting works well. For example, if an account team has scheduled a meeting with one of their clients, you might be able to conduct a short session discussing the client's needs in the area of interest. Following this, you could schedule a few one-on-one interviews with participants of the meeting or with direct users. Such a plan would suit the expectations of the sales team, while gathering the necessary detailed field data, thereby making prospective customers feel listened to by their software vendor.

Prototyping the Design Solution

With the value proposition in place, at least as a theory, you need to communicate and test it. The universal common language of corporations seems to be PowerPoint slideshows, and that's often the best first representation of a new idea. Alternatively, HTML prototypes can create a "clickable" experience at a minimum cost to development.

Based on knowledge gathered from research and data collected from whatever customer visits the design team could do, developing a rough design solution is the next step. The customer visits provide information about people's real needs; the UI building blocks provide standard solutions to common problems. By putting the two together, you can come up with a reasonable first cut at a solution.

Management can use the prototype to evaluate the business proposition and decide whether to go forward. Marketing can use the prototype as a demo to test the waters with potential customers and development partners, which can make it easier to set up interviews later. And the design team itself uses the prototype to firm up its ideas and develop the prototype to take out to real users for testing (see Chapter 6 for situations where this is appropriate).

The SAP xPD Proof of Concept

One of the SAP xPD team members had practical experience with early product-concept development. The team combined his knowledge with its understanding of the UI building blocks and with experience from previous SAP xApps and SAP NetWeaver Portal projects to generate a prototype of a possible solution. The prototype itself was a click-through mock-up providing a fairly realistic portrayal of what an innovation management solution might eventually look like and how it might behave at runtime.

The prototype won management buy-in. It was shown to key customers by marketing, which resulted in strong interest from several. This was critical in helping the group set up field interviews for gathering essential customer data.

2.4   Project Activities

One important success factor is to build a team that is cross-functional. You should ensure that all people who need to define, design, and build the application have a clear understanding of the users' needs and can contribute their expertise to understanding the data. A team may have core members as well as adjunct members who participate in some key activities.

Each project should start with an assessment of the innovation level and the amount of investigation and design needed to develop the application. This estimate will determine the effort you need to spend in each step of the design process. As the project proceeds, especially in the problem analysis phase, this assessment will have to be redefined continuously.

The typical steps of the adapted Contextual Design process are described briefly here. The chapters that follow describe them fully.

1. **Problem Analysis**
   The problem is investigated through literature review, market research, and interviews with stakeholders to determine business goals, high-level process, and obvious pain points.

2. **Prototype**
   An initial design is created to demonstrate the general idea and the potential benefit of an application to both internal management and key potential customers. For quick turnaround, the design is based on existing building blocks. Ideally, a few Contextual Interviews are run to provide initial data for this prototype.

3. **Contextual Interviews**
   The core field-data-gathering process of Contextual Design is based on one-on-one interviews with direct and indirect users, observing them perform their work, and discussing the implications with them. Interviews are debriefed during interpretation sessions in which interviewers, along with other team members, capture all insights and work models. For some projects, interview results are consolidated into a single view representing all the work patterns, intents, strategies, and other elements from the individual work models.

4. **Visioning**
   The group reviews customer data collected by the team and responds with an invention of new work practices that incorporate technology and process ideas, including building on the design patterns.

5. **Mapping to UI Building Blocks and UI Design**
   Similar to use-case analysis, the team creates scenarios or pictorial storyboards that allow the design team to work through the details of the new work practice and provide insight into how it can be supported with the UI building blocks. This helps the team identify what

screens and data are needed to support the envisioned work practice. Storyboards and context maps grounded in field data can align system design with work practice and help bridge the gap between requirements gathering and UI design.

6. **Prototyping and Prototype Interviews**

To test a design before it is actually built, prototypes can be created first in paper and later as an online prototype as the design takes shape. Paper prototypes are quick to create, easy to change while with users, and encourage users to work through their own tasks, interacting with and modifying the prototype as they go along.

These project activities define the parts of the recommended design process for composite applications, based on the type of project. The different types of project (streamlining, surfacing, and inventing) each follow a slightly different sequence of these steps, but they are all borrowing from the same basic structure. Figure 2.1 shows the different activities and how they fit together.

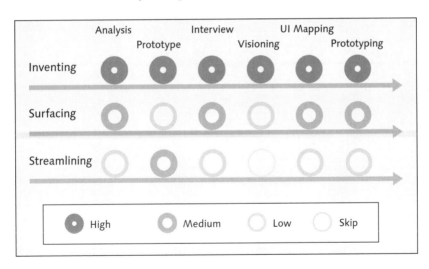

Figure 2.1 Different Design Roadmaps Depending on the Project Scope

The table in this figure represents idealized processes. In reality, whenever an understood work practice matches a building block closely, you can map it directly and create prototypes of the building block, as in the streamlining case. Whenever new processes must be designed, you need to slow down and use more detailed data to drive the design, as in the inventing case. A real project will have some elements that are well understood and others that require new design. We expect each team to adapt these processes to their particular needs as they determine how much they reliably know about their users and their processes.

3   Requirements Gathering

An application is always part of a larger work practice. It is used in the context of other tools and manual processes. Composite application design always involves the redesign of work practice, leveraging new technology to better support and transform the practice. Having a positive impact on work practice is the key goal of all projects. An IT project that has no impact on the work practice is probably not worth the effort. A software product that doesn't improve the way people are working is probably not worth the money.

Work practice simply cannot be designed well if it is not understood in detail. The question is, "What kind of detail?" A high-level process model shows the large organizational steps of a business practice, but not the lower-level steps that people take to run the process and to interact with each other. The work practice of people participating in a process is often neglected. It is this low-level detail about daily life that informs the designer what the system needs to do and helps the project team to come up with a good application. With this detail, the application can support the needs of individual users and work groups—how to get and use information, organize themselves, use and create reports, and all the other activities that make up the daily life of workers carrying out business processes.

How can you develop this understanding? Designers are seldom experienced in the work they are supporting. And even if they used to do that work in a former life (an argument we often hear), they are no longer doing it in the current business climate, within the current business process, and with the current technology. In the end, each individual represents the experience of only one type of user. And a user who has built the application and learned all about the underlying technology no longer represents an average enterprise user, who has little tolerance for technical complexity and no desire to change his or her normal work style. So, if designers operate from their gut feelings, they rely only on their own experience as a user. If that gut feeling or instinct is more tolerant of technology than average users, it is a poor guide to a successful application.

A good requirements-gathering process must include a process for building an in-depth understanding of how people work and how the current work practice is structured. This will guide imagining what technology might do to improve the work—and those improvements define the requirements on the system. Requirements gathering is not simply a matter of asking people what they need in a system. Users do not fully understand what technology is capable of, and furthermore, they are not aware of what they themselves really do. Because the things people do every day become habitual and unconscious, people can rarely describe their work practice. People are conscious of the high-level work steps of their tasks, and they can certainly say what makes them angry at the system. However, they cannot provide the day-to-day detail about what they are doing that is needed to ground designers in what the practice really entails.

The way to get a system that works for people and the business is to first understand how people work and then generate concrete product features or system ideas. But sometimes designers are presented with design solutions based on a platform or someone else's hot idea. Now the project is in "hypothesis mode." Stakeholders assume that certain features would turn this composite application into a killer app or at least be competitive. Under these conditions, don't abandon data collection. The purpose of interviewing users now becomes a matter of validating the design hypotheses. When you feel that most of the product ideas are coming from someone else's gut feeling, don't fight with the stakeholder. Instead, offer to validate the assumptions in the field. This way you simultaneously validate and iterate the design concept and collect additional requirements that will emerge from direct observations and discussions with users.

To ensure that designers get the detailed user data they need to produce high-quality applications, we recommend *Contextual Interviews* as the field-data-gathering process. In this chapter, we introduce the technique of Contextual Interviews and then describe methods for interpreting and modeling the resulting data. In the following chapter, we will address how to *consolidate* that data—how to look across all the users to provide the project team with a visual representation of the entire population's needs, the business process structure, and the tasks that individuals perform. This picture of the real-work practice provides the detailed data you need to reason together with your team members about the existing work practice and invent a new one supported by the composite application. Consolidated data is critical to successful application development.

3.1　Interviewing Users

Contextual Interviews are a field-data-gathering technique in which designers go out into the field and talk with people about their work while they are observing them. When designers watch people while they work, users do not have to articulate their own work practice.

In a Contextual Interview, you conduct a one- to two-hour interview with a user of the proposed design. During the interview, the interviewee does work tasks related to the design problem while you observe. You discuss aspects of the work practice that seem particularly interesting or relevant to the design. In this way, the interview reveals motivations, preferences, exception conditions, and special cases that might not occur during the interview itself. The user can retell (and often replay) interesting tasks that happened in the recent past to illustrate these other situations. The user's body language and emotional reaction are cues to what matters in the work. As much as possible, the interviewer keeps the user grounded in actual events and real cases.

For example, in an interview with a product manager, she describes how the company has set up in general the process of driving new product ideas. To get to a much more detailed level, we asked her about her most current product concept development and walked through some concrete work artifacts, like the consolidated list of new requirements for the next product release, that can be used to retell what has happened in the recent past. In this way, we discovered who was involved in this preparation and what role the user played.

Each interview will result in very detailed data about that part of the work process that the user does and that was observed during the interview. Users may describe how their coworkers do things, but that information will necessarily be much more high-level and limited by the perspective of the user being interviewed. Later in the process, information from all users will be consolidated so the holes in the data from one user can be filled with detailed data from other users.

During the interview, you take notes to capture the findings. Notes are handwritten in a notebook, thereby keeping the complexity of running the interview to a minimum. You capture everything possible about what the user does and says. Later these notes will guide the interpretation session where key issues and implications are pulled out by the team.

To be prepared for mapping requirements to UI building blocks, you should pay attention to such aspects of work practice as:

▶ *Actions* taken by the user

▶ Primary work *responsibilities* and key tasks in which the user participates

▶ *Triggers* (events) that initiate or serve as a stimulus for the user's work; for example, exceptions, task assignments, requests, alerts, and so on

▶ *Work lists* that are generated by the system or by the work process that the user has to perform as part of his or her responsibilities

▶ *Collaborative work sequences* that have dependencies on other actors for their completion

▶ The *owner* of a collaborative work sequence

▶ *Interruptions* to the work, whether by phone, email, or in person

▶ *Work objects* or *artifacts* that the user consumes, produces, or references as part of his or her responsibilities and collaborative work

▶ *Watch lists*, key work objects, or activities that the user is constantly monitoring

▶ *Problems* in the work

▶ *Design ideas* shared and discussed during the interview

Throughout, you are thinking about the UI building blocks and whether they are appropriate for supporting the work practice. During an interview, you pay attention to the tasks and processes the application will support. But, if a building block is indicated, your focus can shift to collecting the data required for that building block.

The interviewer's focus is also affected by the type of project:

3.1.1 Streamlining

A streamlining project simplifies and shortens the design cycle by moving directly from initial prototype to iteration with customers. This is possible because in a streamlining project the work is reasonably well understood—legacy systems already support it, but support it poorly or inefficiently. The team also has the UI building blocks, which define appropriate design solutions for a variety of work-practice situations. Putting these two together, you can develop a reasonable first cut at the design solution. You can do a mock up of this design in paper (a process described in Chapter 6) and test it with users on their first interviews.

Interviewers can also combine field interviewing with paper mock-up testing techniques in a hybrid interview that simultaneously explores the users' work practice and tests the initial prototype. Interviewers should spend roughly the first half of their initial interviews running it as a standard Contextual Interview. Over the course of this inquiry, the interviewer learns enough about the user's work to know how that user might use the prototype. The interviewer introduces the prototype after getting a good overview of the user's tasks and fit to the prototype. Then the behavior represented by the prototype is tested with the user, as described in Chapter 6. In this way, you collect both basic observational data about the work practice and get immediate feedback on the provisional design.

The interviewer may discover that an important task in the work was not considered, or was not well understood during the initial prototype. The interviewer may find out that work that was thought to be supported by a legacy system is actually done using informal, poorly understood procedures. An initial prototype will not support such tasks well. In this instance, the interviewer spends more time using the Contextual Interview approach to understand the nature of these tasks, returning to the prototype when the user returns to tasks that were better anticipated. Should you discover that most of the work is not, in fact, well understood, you may need to change your design approach to one appropriate for a surfacing project.

3.1.2 Surfacing

A surfacing project has two focuses for the data it collects. First, the design team needs data that reveals the whole work process being surfaced, across all players and departments. Second, the detailed data of individual work practice reveals the structure of individual tasks, guiding the eventual development of specific tools. The team runs interviews with the primary users of the proposed system and possibly also with people who work directly with them, such as managers and those providing input to the system.

Interviewers focus on how users participate in the current practice for the business process of interest, and on their use of tools and self-organization techniques that get the work done. When desktop tools such as Microsoft Office are used heavily, the interviewer looks at how documents and spreadsheets are structured and why users rely on them. They pay attention to the ways existing system applications and desktop tools support collaboration, self-organization, and data reporting. The structure and intent of the artifacts people manipulate reveal the needs of the work and suggest potential system work objects. For example, we discovered in one surfacing project that the "sticky notes" feature of Adobe Acrobat Reader was at the core of collaboration for web content management. This helped drive innovations into our solution that tested extremely well in prototype trials with work group users.

Typically, an interviewer will not have an initial prototype for a surfacing interview. But a prototype may have been built as part of the initial business case. If it fits the work well, the team can use it in the first round of interviewing just as in the streamlining project—bringing it out once the work is understood, seeing if it supports the work practice, and abandoning it if it does not. Just make sure you get the basic work practice data first.

3.1.3 Inventing

In an inventing project, the entire data collection process can take longer as the team covers the key users and stakeholders in the planned process. It's not possible to reinvent or introduce important new business processes with only a few interviews, and skipping key stakeholders can undermine change management. Remember that a Contextual Interview is an excellent way to ensure that the users feel heard by the company producing the application.

When inventing, there's no best practice to be studied—the new practice will become the next best practice. The team's goal in gathering data is to understand the structure of the business and the needs of the people in the business. They should interview not only the primary users of the system, but secondary users and key collaborators of the primary users. People upstream or downstream in the process may have valuable perspectives. The design team may talk to suppliers or customers in other industries with similar business practices. This allows the process designers to "get outside" the work and consider solutions such as changes to the basic original equipment manufacturer (OEM) or subcontractor relationship.

If a new practice is being introduced, the design team looks for parallel work practices or business processes already in place, so they can understand how to create the best structure for the new practice. For example, if the product innovation design team wanted to explore using an open community to define requirements and product concepts, they could look at the feedback loop in the open systems community: how influence councils and user groups work, what information is exchanged between end users and development, how the role of internal IT is impacted, and other aspects of the development of ideas through community forums.

Contextual Interviews with users within the business process and those in related processes produce a much richer set of data that looks broadly at the whole work practice. This wide scope is appropriate for driving real innovation, but is overkill for a simpler project.

Remember, though, that projects may combine aspects of all three types of projects. Some practices may be well-defined and understood; others may be handled by implicit, undefined procedures; and still others may require totally new work process invention. Pay attention to the particular problems and shift tactics as necessary.

3.2   Interpreting the Data

A Contextual Interview results in lots of unstructured handwritten notes. You record these notes during the interview to capture what the user was doing, their intents, their motivations, and the role of systems.

To consolidate and draw design implications, this raw data needs to be shared with the team, structured into work models, and analyzed for key issues.

Without analysis, the understandings of individual interviewers would remain unarticulated and tacit. They might develop a "gut feeling" for what users need, but they would find it hard to support that feeling with convincing arguments. Interviewers need to say what they found and they need to share those findings with the team. This generates a common understanding of the issues among team members. With this shared understanding, the team can agree on a common response.

Finally, it's important to represent the structure of work practice explicitly. Systems are built for a user population, not for individuals. Showing the work practice with work models enables the team to see the structure of the users' work.

Therefore, the team needs a forum and a process to make sense of the data and construct it into a reusable format:

▶ *Interpretation sessions* provide the context for debriefing each Contextual Interview. Interpretation sessions should be held within 48 hours of the actual interview.

▶ *Work models* provide a notation to capture and illustrate aspects of work practice in an explicit way that can be shared and communicated.

▶ *Observational notes* are used to capture all important observations, insights, ideas, or breakdowns that are worth mentioning and that should not be lost.

You'll need to choose a method for interpreting the data from your interviews. This interpretation gives you the opportunity to decide what you learned from the interviews. Make sure you allow enough time for interpretation, after all, there's no point in doing the interview if you don't have time to understand what it means. Our rule of thumb is that it takes an hour of interpretation time for every hour of observation.

Here are some options for data interpretation:

3.2.1 The Team Interpretation Session

The most powerful way of interpreting the data is to have the entire team do it together. We recommend that a team be cross-functional, if possible, to pull on different skills when looking at the data: developers, UI designers, documentation writers, and user experience professionals. A team may be as small as two people or as large as six. Teams larger than this risk communication and coordination problems.

In the interpretation session, the interviewer walks through the events of the interview from his or her notes, going in order and skipping nothing. One team member writes down all these key insights and issues raised by the team in their discussion—these points will feed the affinity diagram later (CDTools[1] makes this process simple).

---

1 CDTools™ is InContext's software tool designed specifically to help you organize, analyze, track, and share user data. For more information, go to *www.incontextdesign.com*.

During the team interpretation session, everyone learns about the interview at the same time. Team members hear each others' reactions and can respond to and expand on them. For example, the interviewer reports how the product manager called a colleague asking who might help her to get in touch with a material expert for getting information about the technical feasibility of a new idea. This exchange of facts leads team members to insights about their problems. They now know that assessing technical feasibility is part of the evaluation of a new idea.

During this process of capturing the key facts and their implications, the team may also come up with design ideas. For example, the system might invent an "expert finder," or a guided procedure to standardize the criteria for evaluation. In this way, the team comes to a common understanding of the customer's problem and the design focus, which makes designing the solution much easier.

The team is also capturing the observed work practice in the form of coherent work models, each focusing on certain characteristics, analogous to responsibilities users have or task sequences users perform.

One team member captures the roles or flow model, writing job titles, responsibilities, and flow of communication between all players as the data is discussed. Another member writes the steps that the user takes to accomplish a task. We will introduce these models in more detail in the next chapter.

We recommend that notes be captured on a computer and displayed on the wall for all to see and check for accuracy. Models are drawn on flip charts or captured online and displayed, if simple lists. Work artifacts are circulated and archived for later reference in the design. All notes and models are tagged with a unique user code to preserve the user's confidentiality, such as "U8" for the eighth user. Everyone has a job to do, and everyone is focused on the data from the user.

In capturing the sequence model, we recommend that you record the steps at whatever level of detail the interviewer discovered them, as long as the sequence is in the project focus. The resulting sequence will be uneven—high-level and sketchy in places, very detailed in others. Later, during consolidation, the sequences will be cleaned up and the "swim-lane" layout will be used to show which actors perform each part of the sequence.

Interpretation sessions may be run with two to six team members, allowing teams to split up and run interpretation sessions concurrently to accelerate the process. In this case, the teams must share resulting models, insights, and issues to ensure they maintain a shared understanding of the data and its implications.

3.2.2 Individual Interpretation

Individual interpretation may go faster, but that's in part because you get less data. The team doesn't have the opportunity to discuss the implications of the data with each other, which can limit the identification of additional issues. This is the trade-off you have to make.

So what do you do if you are very restricted for time, or simply don't have the people you need to work together? If you do have a team experienced in interviewing, interpreting as a team, and data consolidation, you may have team members interpret their own data. This is best done after a few interpretation sessions have been completed together, so that all team members have begun to develop a shared understanding of the problem. You can also do this with at least one other team member to give an outside point of view.

After these group sessions, interviewers review their own notes; identify key points; record roles (described in the next section), responsibilities, and work artifacts; and write out sequence models (defined below). The team meets regularly to hear about the interviews others have conducted, and reviews the results of the interviews. Individual interpretations may take longer since each interviewer must now record his or her own observations and all the models.

If you decide to run such an accelerated interpretation process, the team must be more experienced. Keep the different types of information—facts, interpretations, key issues, design ideas, and work models—all separate so you can consolidate the data more easily at a later time. Even experienced teams working individually will produce fewer insights and will take longer to produce a shared understanding. To some extent, you will have to invest the necessary time to communicate all the findings to the development team – details will have to be explained anyway.

3.2.3 Direct UI Mapping

In a streamlining process, it may be unnecessary to record work models. When an existing, well understood process is being improved, the team can assemble UI building blocks into a solution directly from the interview data.

For example, where the user acts within a larger process, the Guided Procedure building block can be used directly; and where the user is working on an individual work artifact, an object-instance view is the appropriate building block to use. The interviewer can fill in the building block with the specific data from the interview, resulting in a customized UI for that user. A quick step of reconciling differences across users leads to a prototype design that is ready for testing.

Beyond filling in the building block, you may have additional observations that you want to capture to characterize needs and practices. In this case, run your interpretation session to capture the issues, but fill in the building blocks as you go.

Whichever aforementioned method you select, make sure you share findings with the other team members to ensure that you are creating a shared team understanding of what the users need and what might be built with the UI building blocks.

SAP xPD: The Customer Blitz

The SAP xApp Product Definition (SAP xPD) team needed to gather field data about their problem, but had limited corporate buy-in and funding for this activity. They invented the "customer blitz" to overcome the problem.

The goal of a customer blitz is to get a quick understanding of a business process, gather data in a short period of time, and fit this into planned corporate visits. The key to its success is getting real, detailed data about the users' work, ensuring that the perspectives of the team are incorporated into the data interpretation, and maintaining a shared understanding of users' needs.

When the marketing and sales organization sets up a corporate visit to a key customer, a customer blitz can be added to that visit. This is an especially useful structure for the initial data gathering while building the business case. If the team has only a short time to collect a lot of data or wants to go to geographically distant locations, a "blitz" is a good way to gather and interpret data within one week. Moreover, if a project needs to cover many roles in a large process, a blitz may be the optimal way to move quickly.

The SAP xPD team started their blitz with a larger meeting of all stakeholders. This meeting provided key stakeholders and management the opportunity to air their concerns and requirements. During this meeting, the team developed an understanding of the overall process flow, using the contributions of all present.

This high-level roadmap gave the team context for understanding the detailed data and helped to ensure that no part of the process was forgotten. From here, the team identified key users to interview with Contextual Interviews.

Then they split up and conducted Contextual Interviews one-on-one with the primary roles in the workflow. (When there are many roles, the goal should be to get data from at least two people in each core role.) For the first few interviews with central roles, the team interpreted as a group to give everyone an overview of the issues and the process.

After initial interpretations, the team accelerated the process by allowing interviewers to interpret as individuals. Each interviewer wrote down the key issues, tasks, roles, and responsibilities relevant to the problem and projected solution. They met regularly to review new data and ensure that everyone interpreted the data in the same way, and developed a shared understanding of the users' needs and the roles identified so far.

Another way of approaching interpretation would be to have the team interpret interviews in pairs, ensuring two points of view on the data. In either case, it's especially important when a team works independently to meet regularly; otherwise, it's too easy to lose any common understanding of the users.

When all interviews were interpreted, the SAP xPD team consolidated that data as described in the next chapter.

3.3   Modeling Work Practice

Work models are explicit representations of work practice—of what people do to make the work of the business happen. They are built using the data generated from the Contextual Interviews, so they represent what people actually do, not what is written down in a corporate procedure manual. By making the work practice explicit, work models enable design teams to identify problems, build on strengths, allow for alternative strategies, and ensure that their solutions match the users and the work.

Work models decompose the information contained in interview protocols into different design-relevant views on the work. As we discuss later, work models simplify consolidation across interviews significantly, because insights from one interview can be merged easily with others.

With SAP's business process platform, much of the structure of work practice is built into the UI building blocks themselves. So there's less need for explicit work modeling than there is in an unconstrained design process such as Contextual Design, from which these models are drawn. If the UI building blocks are already built into the development environment, the design depends primarily on the affinity diagram and the flow and the sequence work models. These models are targeted to reveal the detailed aspects of work practice that will drive the instantiation or adaptation of a building block.

3.3.1 Observational Notes

Each field interview reveals new insights and facts about the work practice of users. In addition to capturing work models, certain observations, insights, and design ideas may seem to be of primary importance to the project and should be documented as well. Also, some interview data that doesn't fit well into any of the current work models may still have a great impact on what should be designed.

Observational notes capture these issues. Notes may be observations about the work, identification of different work strategies or intents, or key facts, insights, or design ideas for the team to keep in mind. Notes can cover issues of culture, the impact of the physical environment, overarching problems with technology, the effect of law and standards, and other influencing factors on the work practice. These points are captured as individual notes, one idea to a note.

The SAP xPD project captured observational notes in a simple Microsoft Word document and printed them out on separate sticky notes. The team printed a numbered list containing the numeric identifier for the interviewee and a unique number for the note. Including the numeric identifier can be helpful if questions about the meaning of a note arise during the consolidation of data from all interviews. Or, you can use CDTools to track your users and capture your notes in support of the consolidation step.

Let's look at an example of observational notes. These notes were captured on the SAP xPD project during an interview with an engineering expert (identified as U3).

Observational Notes—U3 Engineering Expert	
U3–1	Process and product development is physically collocated and has one common management, because this work requires intensive collaboration.
U3–2	Innovation requires not just coordination between process and product people, but intensive collaboration (joined meetings, brainstorming, and opportunity identification).
U3–3	There are special initiatives around technology that is protected (with respect to intellectual property) and may be leveraged in other products or processes to establish competitive advantage.
U3–4	The organizational structures used to be along products. Now, it is along key technology.
. . .	

Table 3.1 Observational Notes from an SAP xPD Interpretation Session

Observational notes ensure that the team captures the issues relevant to this population and business process. As we will see in the next chapter, these notes are later sorted into coherent clusters to form an *affinity diagram* that organizes and communicates important issues about the market targeted by the application. Capturing individual notes makes this later organization possible.

3.3.2 Role Analysis

In Contextual Design, the flow model shows people's responsibilities and related work objects in the domain of interest, and also shows communication and coordination among people. When consolidated, this is the key model for understanding the overall business and for redesigning organizational and group process. But for most composite applications, the role analysis is sufficient to drive redesign. Here we introduce the concepts of the flow model and discuss how it can be used.

A *role* is a collection of responsibilities that, taken together, create a job profile that a person performs. People play many roles when they do their work. The key to design is defining those roles. A *responsibility* is a duty that the user performs as a part of his or her job, or as part of a business process, whether officially assigned or informally taken on. Responsibilities may be apparent through direct observation during the interview, or may be captured as the intent behind several behaviors. For example, one interviewee helped a new group member write a technical disclosure form, taught a class to new hires on the concept patent process, and led discussion lunches on special topics. These actions might be generalized to the responsibility "mentors junior inventors."

Work objects are the things that the user manipulates, creates, references, receives, or passes along. They often become the content of the UI building blocks. Artifacts are often the nouns in the responsibility descriptions. In the example above, the invention disclosure form is the artifact and the "invention" is a typical candidate to be modeled as a work object.

Flow lines represent the communication and coordination among people. Flow lines are the passing of a work artifact or information from one person to another or a discussion between people. Passing the invention disclosure form to legal and subject matter experts is an example of such a flow line.

The flow model may be captured with or without flow lines. If the project is addressing a coherent work group and does not intend to restructure the communication within that work group, flow lines can be omitted. But if coordination is a major concern, if the project crosses work group boundaries, or if the work practice is likely to be significantly restructured, then it is important to see the communication among people. In that case, the team should capture the flow lines.

As an example from the SAP xPD project, one interview of an engineering expert produced these roles:

Roles—U3 Engineering Expert	
Work Responsibilities	▶ Leads innovation projects that create *feasibility reports* or *engineering design reports* (about three projects at one time, such as the new widget machine)
	▶ Is expert for widget machines
	▶ Coordinates with people (product, process, and material) that are related to that technology
	▶ Invents new *concepts* and documents them in *patent notebook*
	▶ Writes and submits *invention disclosure forms*
	▶ Works with advanced technology groups (widget components)
	▶ Cross coordinates with other sector that is using same technology
	▶ Gives classes on widget making and widget technology
	▶ Is member of the five-year technology strategy team for his sector
	▶ Creates technical reports
	▶ Reviews technical reports
	▶ Stays up to date with recent development by going to trade shows
Work Objects	▶ Feasibility report
	▶ Engineering design report
	▶ Concept
	▶ Patent notebook
	▶ Invention disclosure form for technical report

Table 3.2 Work Responsibilities and Work Objects from an SAP xPD Project Interview

The SAP xPD team chose to capture only roles and responsibilities in a simple textual list. Had they chosen to capture flow lines as well, they would have produced a more graphical representation (see Figure 3.1).

As shown in Figure 3.1, U3 passes the work object *Technical Report* to another engineering group and receives technical reports from them. He delivers training to new coworkers, and updates his patent notebook. He also coordinates with technology experts in unstructured conversations.

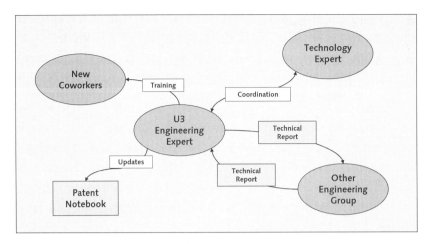

Figure 3.1 The Full Contextual Design Flow Model (Responsibilities Omitted for Clarity)

3.3.3 **Task Analysis**

In Contextual Design, the structure of individual or collaborative complex tasks is modeled in the form of sequence models. A sequence model represents the steps of a task ordered in time, potentially across organizational roles, to accomplish business intent. Sequence models answer the question of how a responsibility gets accomplished. For example, "How did the interviewee review a technical disclosure form?" or "How did the interviewee provide a feasibility analysis?" Each sequence model describes a single task, so each interview produces several sequence models.

Sequence models may be represented at several levels of detail. On the most detailed level, an observed work sequence might be the user interaction with a user interface. This sequence is imposed by the navigation structure of the existing system. Be careful with those observations, as they reflect the existing system design (which may be good or bad), but not necessarily the user's preferred way of doing work. You should look for sequences that reflect work practice of individuals or work groups that are driven by actual best practices or domain-specific dependencies of steps.

Formal use cases with actors and system response are not an appropriate tool to capture requirements, because at this point we are interested in user's intent, not the system's response. Sequences represent the users' work behavior, not each step that someone might take with the system. Instead, we capture what they did to get the job done, including the system steps used. In this way, we see the whole work that we can think about redesigning later.

The level of detail you get depends on how close you get to the real work. For example, when you, as an interviewer, see the user perform a task, the sequence tends to be highly detailed, showing each individual work step of the task, including the interaction with the application screen. When you hear only about the task in a retrospective account, sequence steps will describe higher-level actions that cover potentially many detailed work steps. Those high-level actions may map to entire phases within the lifecycle of a work process that can be modeled as phases of a guided-procedure definition, each having a number of actions to accomplish in itself.

Any retrospective account of one person's role in a larger business process should include the source of artifacts, emails, or instructions; to whom artifacts and communications were passed; and descriptions of multiple collaborations. By documenting these sequences, you start to capture the overall business process and include potentially many contributors.

To help you gather all important aspects of individual or collaborative task flows, the sequence model should include the following elements:

▶ **Triggers**

Work sequences have triggers that initiate or serve as a stimulus for the interviewee to begin the work. A trigger may be something explicit and obvious like an email from a manager requesting a technical review. It may also be implicit, as in the case of a weekly project-status report. We classify triggers in the following way:

▷ System-generated exceptions delivered as alerts or notifications

▷ Workflow items generated by standard business workflows, such as a request for approval

- Standard work items generated by the system, such as travel expenses to be cleared or unpaid balances to be reconciled, or coming through email

- Ad-hoc messages from colleagues, such as tasks, requests, informational notifications, questions, announcements, and so on

- The result of users checking out status indicators or analytics, such as those from a report or a dashboard

- Periodic reminders

- Communication from outside the system (phone, front desk, and so on

▶ Work Actors

A given work sequence may involve people other than the interviewee for its successful completion. For example, the work sequence "substantiate product concept" from an SAP xPD interview revealed that staff performing business development, project management, and corporate strategy all contribute in the sequence from the engineering expert's perspective. As a part of our sequence model, we want to capture all the significant parties that play a part in the work sequence as work actors. However, if an actor not only contributes to the current sequence, but starts a new coherent task, then a new sequence should be modeled. In this case, the team notes the handoff from one sequence performed by one actor to another sequence performed by another actor.

▶ Owners

Owners have the overall responsibility for a given work sequence, and this responsibility should be captured on the flow model. In an SAP xPD interview, the marketing research analyst work actor was ultimately accountable for the quality of the findings presentation in the executive summary. In this case, the marketing analyst work actor was the designated owner.

▶ Work Objects

These are the work objects that appear as part of the work sequences. Many may appear on the flow model as well. Note that in our sequence model, we are likely to focus on a small set of primary work objects, some of which transition across various states during the course of the work sequence. For example, a complex quotation might go from being "under construction" to "draft" to "screened" to "approved" to "signed" status during the activities of the work sequence. So, you can use sequence models for getting insights about the key states of business objects and to understand exactly what status triggers what actions. Look for and capture such changes in status to the work objects you identify during the interpretation; they suggest the use of the guided-procedure and object-action patterns later on.

▶ **Activities**

In reality, responsibilities are materialized in the form of discrete tasks or large chunks of concrete work that must be accomplished. Unlike operational workflow, an activity is owned by a single person, and you may observe those at the work place or being described by the interviewee as a work sequence or single task. Activities may be collaborative, sequential, or user-controlled, complex or simple, but the original work intent always provides a well-defined context. Each instance of an activity has local roles assigned to the actors and is monitored by one or several actors.

▶ **Steps**

A step in a work sequence is a discrete unit of work from the perspective of the primary work actor (the interviewee). Steps may be represented at many levels of detail. They can imply many low-level actions like "create concept document," which clearly comprises many detailed system interactions—open the document template, fill in background information, and so on—but can usefully be thought of as a conceptual whole. Or, they can represent the low-level activities themselves, which are important for redesigning the overall user experience and individual optimization. Steps may be grouped together to form higher-order activities. Depending on the redesign you need, you may represent your sequence as a set of high-level steps (activities) or a set of low-level steps grouped into activities. When we string together all of the steps and chunk them into activities associated with a work responsibility, we can see the sequence of the work.

▶ **Breakdowns**

In real work, of course, things go wrong: a database crashes, a work actor forgets to perform a review, a customer inadvertently omits an important piece of information in an order, and so on. Because information about such breakdowns can provide valuable insights to the designer, we explicitly capture them as a part of the sequence model.

Here's an example of a sequence model built by the SAP xPD team. In the following high-level sequence model (see Table 3.3), with work objects in italics, each step represents a complete activity. These individual sequence models can be quite simple, with a minimum of formalism, since they are consolidated into more structured versions later.

U8—Marketing Research Analyst—Initiating a Market Study	
Purpose	Product manager creates *research request*
Trigger	Research request sent to U8
Step	U8 reviews research request
Breakdown	Research request lacks detailed attribute and focus information
Step	U8 solicits detailed information from product manager
Step	Product manager provides research request details
Step	On receiving details, U8 requests *study* approval of the marketing manager
Step	Marketing manager approves study
Step	U8 selects demographic segment and focus
Step	U8 chooses appropriate study method
Breakdown	Poor knowledge sharing between product management and marketing research
Step	U8 writes project request

Table 3.3 An Individual High-Level Sequence Model from the SAP xPD Project

U8—Marketing Research Analyst—Initiating a Market Study	
Step	U8 initiates project with vendor
Step	Vendor conducts study, producing the *study results*
Step	U8 interprets the results
Breakdown	No single place to capture ideas or issues
Step	U8 creates and distributes *executive summary* of study

Table 3.3 An Individual High-Level Sequence Model from the SAP xPD Project (cont.)

3.3.4 Advanced Analysis

Observational notes, formal flow models, or just a list of roles and sequence models are sufficient to characterize users' work practice for most composite application projects. B, if the project warrants it—if the work to be changed is complex, or if the population to be supported is unknown to the design team—the team may choose to abstract out more detailed data by using the additional Contextual Design models.

▶ The *cultural model* captures the influences and influencers in the markets. It shows perception of the current technology, experience of the business process, pain points, and the effect of standards, law, geographic culture, organizational values, power, and interpersonal friction. When consolidated, the cultural model reveals the key value proposition for the target population. For example, the innovation management team found tension between the different stakeholders who all claim ownership of product vision. It is marketing, development, business analysts, and user researchers who want to influence the product. System design may address this and come up with ideas of helping to balance those different perspectives and create synergy.

▶ The *physical model* captures the physical environment, how space and desktop are used, issues of distributed work, and workflow within the workspace itself. The desk, seat of a car, or bookshelf show the natural clustering and organizing of work, and reveal the concepts by which people organize themselves.

- The *artifact model* captures the things, physical and virtual, that people use for completing their work, such as documents, notes, web pages, email, and wall displays. When consolidated, the artifact model reveals the data and layout that needs to be designed for an online artifact. It is the model of the work objects that are key to the business process being supported. In product innovation management, patent disclosure forms, actual submissions of ideas, or the Excel spreadsheet representing the prioritized list of requirements, are all very helpful in understanding what matters to users.

3.4 Variations in Handling Requirements Gathering

The project structures we introduced earlier suggest different approaches to the data collection and interpretation processes, depending on the innovation level of the project.

- **Streamlining**

  A streamlining project is likely to adopt the last option for handling interpretation—a direct mapping from interviews to UI building blocks. In such a project, the expectation is that because the team will be familiar with the building blocks provided by the platform, they will move to design quickly. So it is likely to build an initial prototype and test it through hybrid interviews. The team may well choose to capture key issues and consolidate them into an affinity diagram to organize and highlight key issues, but might not capture any other work models. When a building block has been identified for use, individual team members can abstract out the necessary data for the building block before the interpretation session. The interpretation session focuses on issues of the work practice outside of the prototype, or related to the response to the prototype itself (as we discuss in Chapter 6, which describes the interpretation session for a mock-up interview).

- **Surfacing**

  Surfacing projects are more complex because the process is not as well understood as streamlining projects. The team will capture key issues and responsibilities of core roles for the key members of the target work group. They will also capture the sequence model to show a hand-off of work objects and collaboration between users.

▶ **Inventing**

Projects that reinvent whole business practices or introduce wholly new practices are the most difficult and most risky. For these projects, other Contextual Design models like the cultural, physical, and artifact models might be useful as well, in addition to the issues and flow and sequence models. In an inventing project, it's worthwhile to develop the fullest possible understanding of the work practice. If the process is large and involves many players, the team may use a "customer blitz" process to get a quick overview of the process and data. Later, more in-depth Contextual Interviews will round out the data and provide the needed detail for the primary and secondary users. An inventing project team should do its interpretation sessions collectively to capitalize on the many perspectives that the full team can offer.

4   Seeing the Big Picture

Each interpretation session produces observational notes, a flow model variant, and a set of sequence models for each user. But to see the issues relevant to your project across your user population, you need a way to pull the data together. You need to transfer findings from all individual interviews into one big picture that reflects the market needs, *without* losing the detail that informs the design of the applications.

This is different from consolidating quantitative data that can simply be transformed into statistics. Interview data is qualitative and requires special techniques.

Teams have been known to produce 200 pages of interview notes, so that each project member has had to read through all the pages and build his or her own opinion of the overall requirements. The consolidation is delegated to the reader. This is not only inefficient but ineffective—interview reports do not easily make for a coherent market view.

We have seen product managers create long lists of use cases derived from all interviews, with each use case justifying one feature request. Such lists do not communicate the big picture. Developers processing and prioritizing such lists of features and use cases no longer have access to the original roles and work practice. Although use cases are a well accepted method of deriving features, thinking about features prematurely is likely to dominate the use cases when it comes time for implementation, if no other information is available. Such feature-based approaches fragment the user experience, because the use cases tend to communicate selected feature ideas and not realistic work-practice scenarios. User interaction cannot be tested because the team no longer has information about the original context in which the tasks are done.

The trick to make this consolidation process streamlined is to first separate the data into independent work models or perspectives, and to consolidate them independently of each other. Each consolidated model gives a coherent perspective on the data and, when viewed collectively, these consolidated models provide a complete picture of the whole user population.

▶ *Flow models* can be consolidated by merging the roles and flow structure into one consolidated flow, and merging responsibilities from identical roles into one consolidated role.

▶ *Sequence models* can be consolidated by merging similar sequences from different interviews into one consolidated sequence for each task.

▶ *Observational notes* can be sorted into clusters, consisting of notes that describe a similar fact or are related to the same topic. The result is called an *affinity diagram* because the notes are sorted based on their affinity to each other.

▶ *UI building blocks* can be consolidated by merging content and functions from all interviews while eliminating duplicates. The result is a more representative instantiation of the building block.

These techniques are most powerful if applied in combination with one another. They give designers multiple views on the work practice as it exists, in the form of consolidated work models or a consolidated design of a UI building block.

The interpretation of each interview is integral to generating rich observational notes and work models. The consolidation across interviews is key to understanding the big picture and informing the design with reliable data representing the requirements of the whole business practice. As interviews with users are conducted and interpreted, the consolidation process captures the common work practice incrementally, rolling each new user into the evolving picture of the work as a whole.

Data consolidation brings together the individual data to make up a set of consolidated models showing common issues, common work patterns and strategies, common ways of organizing work into roles, common obstacles or breakdowns people encounter in their work, and the variations and exceptions to all of these. The team can design the application to address the needs of the whole process, the whole population, or the whole market. They can shift their focus from individual features to the needs of the process and the population.

The extent to which formal consolidation is necessary depends on the complexity of the project; a simple streamlining project can omit most of these activities, while a complex inventing project requires a careful consolidation process. In this chapter, we'll first introduce the different consolidation processes and then discuss when each process is most likely to be needed.

4.1 Building the Affinity Diagram

The affinity diagram is a hierarchical organization of interview observations that shows the scope of issues across all interviews. It reveals what matters for a whole organization or market. A full affinity diagram can include upwards of 1,000 individual notes, organized into groups and themes so that the information is accessible to designers. These groupings show key aspects of work, domains of concern within the work, and important concepts used to organize work. Furthermore, the affinity diagram shows design teams the real scope of the problem from the perspective of users, as well as holes in the data—where more data needs to be gathered or where the project focus needs to be widened. By collecting all the issues from all interviews into a single, coherent structure, designers can see the scope of the issues that they must address.

Driving Innovation	
We need to share know-ledge.	▶ We want to know who is responsible for what, and who is expert on what.
	▶ We would like to document everything to make it available for others.
	▶ We would like to stay up to date with new reports.
	▶ We should have a single point of entry for ideas, issues, insights, and customer feedback.

Table 4.1 A Portion of the SAP xApp Product Definition (SAP xPD) Affinity Diagram

Driving Innovation	
We need to manage the innovation process.	▶ We assign people to tasks, depending on the phase of the innovation process. ▶ We need templates to optimize our work. ▶ We determine the concept leader, depending on the type of innovation. ▶ We prepare reports, documents, and graphics for each approval.
Formal processes sometimes conflict with innovation.	▶ We need people who work with ideas that do not belong to existing categories. ▶ We need to be able to insert good ideas into running development (for example, competencies and resources). ▶ We should have access to valuable information related to product innovation, despite confidentiality issues.

Table 4.1 A Portion of the SAP xApp Product Definition (SAP xPD) Affinity Diagram (cont.)

The affinity diagram is built through a bottom-up, inductive reasoning process. Inductive reasoning, from the particular note to the general issue, creates new insight into the issues in the work practice. You start by printing out all of the individual affinity data notes across all the teams' interpretations. Then, notes that have an affinity for one another—that seem to be about the same work issue—are placed into small groupings on a wall.

A simple color scheme keeps the affinity diagram organized. Start with blue labels to organize the individual notes. Then use pink labels to group the blues. Finally, green labels collect pinks into overarching themes that are of significance in the data. For most affinities, these three layers of groupings are all that's needed to organize individual groups of four to six notes each. In the first version of the affinity, teams may find that smaller groupings of one to three notes let them elevate the important issues. As more data is collected, these groupings expand and may need to be divided to ensure that issues are not buried. Remember that the goal in building an affinity diagram is to get all necessary information in the labels, thereby providing a quick summary across hundreds of notes.

Group labels, written from the point of view of the user, highlight new information in the data. Start by creating blue labels. Avoid using labels that simply name an issue that is already known, such as "usability problems." Instead, use labels to express new insight into the work practice. Also, the labels summarize the information in the individual notes: "We use piles to organize our work," rather than "how we organize our work," for example. The result is that the affinity diagram promotes new insight, with the users telling the design team what they need to consider.

After the team has collected and interpreted data from about six users, you are ready to build the first cut of an affinity. At this point, the team may have collected 400 to 600 notes. With this number of notes, and six to ten people to build it, the affinity diagram can be built in one day or less. The affinity building process is a good time to involve stakeholders who may not be doing the interviewing and interpretation work. By building the affinity diagram, business owners, marketing, development, documentation, and (in internal projects) key customers can become familiar with the data and see the kind of issues that are surfacing.

Once the first affinity diagram is built, you add to it as you conduct further interviews. We recommend that you add notes in half-day team sessions dealing with several hundred notes at a time. This ensures that time spent on the affinity is limited to these group sessions; otherwise, the team may continuously massage the affinity. The group event lets you bring others into the sessions as helpers, thereby exposing more people to the data.

Once the affinity is structured in the first session, each new set of notes is used to expand existing groups or create new groups, new labels, and new sections of the wall. As new notes go up, the team may pull notes from existing groupings and restructure the wall to highlight new issues.

The most important use of the affinity diagram is to drive design thinking based on valid data points. The final affinity diagram provides a fast introduction to the issues for the project represented in the voice of the customer. In preparation for the visioning session (see Chapter 6), the team walks the labels of the affinity, reading from top to bottom. As they read, they ask "If this is what's going on with people in this process, what can we build in our application?" This question encourages the team to focus on generating design solutions that fit with the data, transform the work practice, and reuse relevant UI building blocks.

The affinity is useful for general communication to others. Teams have made it widely available to all stakeholders by printing it on plotters to create moveable walls that can be shared with stakeholders. Even the original paper affinity diagram can be built on large sheets of butcher paper, which makes it possible to take it down and transport it for project reviews. Putting the affinity diagram online allows it to be shared across the company and with partners. Consider using CDTools to help you quickly put the affinity diagram online and then publish it to an HTML browser.

Finally, this diagram provides the structure to create an executive report or slideshow. Collect key insights by picking the most surprising or interesting second-level themes and describe them by listing third-level labels as the customer voice. There is a good chance that some of the issues are new, because the affinity diagram was constructed from the bottom up without being constrained by assumptions and stereotypes.

4.2   Consolidating Roles and Flow Model

The consolidated flow model identifies the key roles involved in doing the work, their responsibilities, and, if flow lines are included, the communication between them. Role identification is important, because job descriptions may vary greatly across a market. Even within a business, tasks associated with job titles may change over time. But roles that people play while doing their jobs tend to be very stable. A role has its own coherence that is derived from the job itself. Jobs in organizations aggregate these underlying roles and assign them to people. Designing to the roles, rather than to the individuals, the job title, or personas, ensures the long-term adaptability of a composite application. The UI building blocks provide direct support for an entire role in the form of the Work Center building block that bundles content and functions needed to accomplish all responsibilities of a given role.

The flow model with roles and connecting lines is like a war map, showing the players to target and support. The flow model helps the team see the pattern of relationships between players and reveals opportunities to support collaboration; it shows how responsibilities are clustered into roles that can be supported with specific features, information, or automation; and it reveals artifacts and information that pass between people, which might be supported online.

Role consolidation begins as early as the first customer site visit. The basis of role consolidation is to identify the different *roles* users play. The idea of a role is natural to people. When someone says "I wear several hats," they're saying that they play several roles in their job. Each role has its own distinct responsibilities, intents, issues, and tasks. "I'm a material expert and develop new technology," a user might say, "but I'm also part of a steering committee that approves new product ideas." Two roles and two primary intents suggest distinct responsibilities and tasks. "I have to stay on top of the company's current financial situation," a CFO might say, "but I have a side project of trying to understand how the new accounting rules will affect us." Again, this data suggests two roles and two separate intents.

Roles are identified from the individual role listings for each user by recognizing similar roles across users and then grouping together similar responsibilities. The team identifies roles in the first individual flow model; then they reuse those same roles where possible in looking at the next. As they move from model to model, they develop a stable list of roles with responsibilities that includes the superset of all the responsibilities across the models.

For example, in the SAP xPD project, the engineering expert (U3) listed the following responsibilities:

Role Listing—U3 Engineering Expert	
Work Responsibilities	▶ Leads innovation projects that create feasibility reports or engineering design reports (about three projects at one time, such as the new widget machine)
	▶ Is expert for widget machines
	▶ Coordinates with people (product, process, and material) that are related to that technology
	▶ Invents new concepts and documents them in patent notebook
	▶ Writes and submits invention disclosure forms
	▶ Works with advanced technology groups (widget components)
	▶ Cross-coordinates with other sector that is using same technology
	▶ Gives classes on widget making and widget technology
	▶ Is member of the five-year technology strategy team for his sector
	▶ Creates technical reports
	▶ Reviews technical reports
	▶ Stays up to date with recent developments by going to trade shows

Table 4.2 Responsibilities for Engineering Expert

Each responsibility suggests a role that it serves. Consider the "Leads innovation projects..." work responsibility above. In performing this work, the user supports the creative aspects of the product design process. The responsibility "Works with advanced technology groups" involves helping these groups apply cutting-edge technologies to new product design ideas. These responsibilities seem to be about the same overall work intent and suggest a single work role entitled "innovation driver."

This process of grouping responsibilities into roles continues until all users are interpreted. The roles may be reused across projects and products, so a role collects responsibilities from an increasing number of interviews. The roles become more complete as additional data is collected.

Role Name	Role Description	Responsibility
Innovation Driver (U3, U9, U5)	Persons who drives the generation of ideas	▶ Leads innovation projects (U3) ▶ Works with advanced technology groups (U3) ▶ Guides product exploration and development teams (U9) ▶ Schedules brainstorm session with task forces (U9) ▶ Scans preexisting insights (U9) ▶ Collects ideas (U9) ▶ Generates proposals for new ideas (U9) ▶ Classifies ideas (U5) ▶ Submits ideas to idea portal (U5) ▶ Analyzes consumer data (U5)
Inventor (U3)	Person who creates ideas or develops new concepts	▶ Invents new concepts (U3) ▶ Documents ideas in personal notebook (for patent submission) (U3) ▶ Writes and submits invention disclosure forms (U3) ▶ Cross-coordinates with experts related to his or her invention (U3) ▶ Creates technical reports (U3)
Subject Matter Expert/ Researcher (U2, U3, U6)	Person who is an expert of a certain domain	▶ Reviews technical reports (U2, U3) ▶ Submits technical reports to archive system (U2) ▶ Writes technical reports (U2) ▶ Joins trade shows to stay up to date (U3) ▶ Gives classes for junior employees (U3) ▶ Supervises junior employees (U4) ▶ Moderates new technology or product-related communities (U2) ▶ Leads innovation teams (U2) ▶ Approves invention disclosure forms (U2) ▶ Evaluates ideas related to his or her work (U2)

Table 4.3 A Partial Role List with Responsibilities, from the SAP xPD Project

Role Name	Role Description	Responsibility
		▶ Screens ideas related to his or her work (U2)
		▶ Collect hot ideas that are related to his or her work (for example, about a material) (U2)
		▶ Develops new material (U2)
		▶ Requests information from suppliers (U2)
		▶ Assesses technology and existing patents (U2)
		▶ Generates technology-driven ideas (U2)
		▶ Participates in research meetings and informs about new technology (U6)
Technical Feasibility Checker (U3)	Person who evaluates feasibility of product concept	▶ Delivers recommendations about concept (U3)
		▶ Evaluates a set of technical options (U3)
		▶ Estimates costs for different options (U3)
		▶ Coordinates writing of engineering design report (U3)
		▶ Manages external companies for working on details (drawings and cost estimates) (U3)

Table 4.3 A Partial Role List with Responsibilities, from the SAP xPD Project (cont.)

The role definition in the flow model maintains the user codes both as a quality check and to map the consolidated roles back against the individual job types. Roles that have been identified from only one user's data are tenuous; if they are central to the work, the team would be well advised to gather more data relevant to that goal.

Applications designed to support such work roles are robust: The user who does not have a particular responsibility listed in the role definition today may well be given that responsibility tomorrow. The organization that has assigned two roles to the same person now may well decide to split them in the next restructuring. When a team designs around the role, their design already accounts for these future changes. Roles are critical to successful composite application design and are behind efficient use of the UI building blocks. Roles identify what functions to collect together into Work Centers that support coherent tasks and what Work Centers to collect together into an individual's Control Center; the tasks and work objects that the user needs access to are defined by the role's responsibilities.

Knowing which users play which roles is also critical for detailed design. If a role is played entirely by agents who work in a call center, the designer must know that agents are interrupted continuously and always have a split focus divided between the phone and the screen. Users in this role do not pay full attention to the interface. Designing for a role played by engineers is quite different; their whole job is about focusing and they can handle technical complexity. Moreover, supporting a role that is played by agents and engineers will require great dexterity in reconciling the two user populations, and could result in the design of two separate interfaces.

Full consolidated flow models capture the communication between roles. The full consolidated flow model is a very powerful tool for analyzing whole organizations and the relationships between organizations. For the complex redesign of processes like inventing projects, the full consolidated flow model that shows secondary roles with flow lines can provide the bigger picture needed for redesign. You can start to see the natural work groups in the organization, revealed by the interaction of roles rather than job positions. The complexity of the communication and coordination is revealed. The inefficiencies in the workflow can be tracked back to how people interact and pass work at a more abstract level than is revealed through the task analysis of the swim-lane diagram. As one group leader remarked, "We built a flow model for our own group and it was great. We discovered we have breakdowns on every communication line out of our group!" Once she had a view of her problem, she could address it.

When the team chooses to build a full consolidated flow model, it will have interviewed a wider scope of users and will have more roles to consolidate. The team will also consolidate the flow lines with their associated objects and communications. To do this, the team brings the flow lines from the original models across to the consolidated model.

Consolidated Flow Model -- Energy Trading

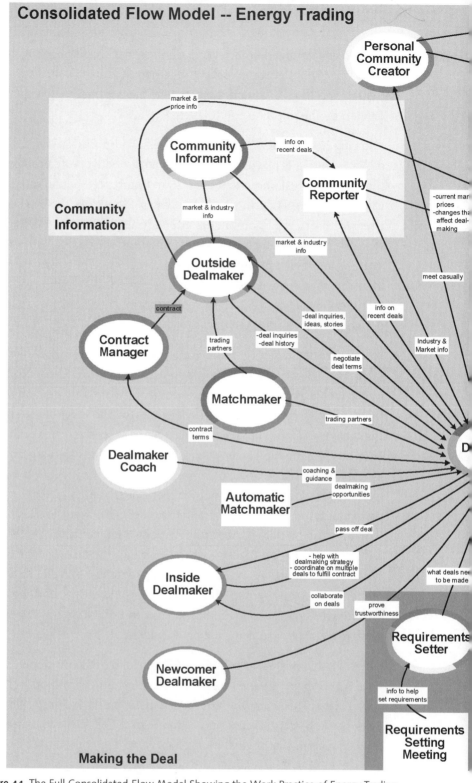

Figure 4.1 The Full Consolidated Flow Model Showing the Work Practice of Energy Trading

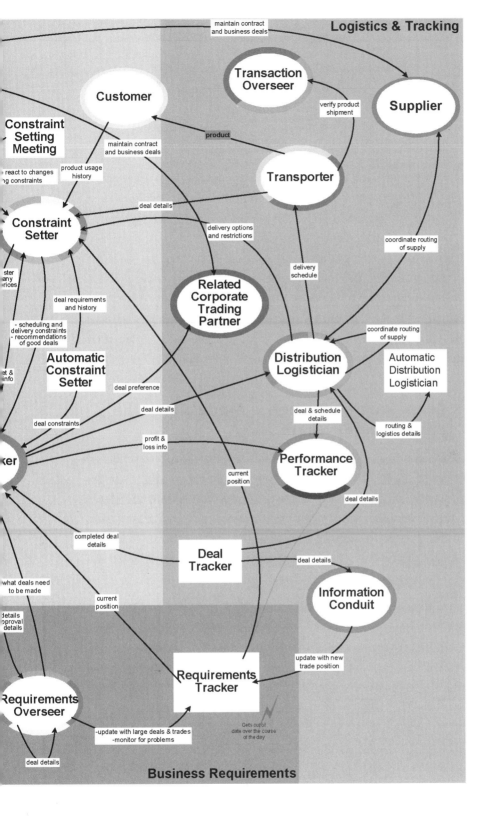

Where two roles communicate or coordinate in one user's situation, those two roles are shown to communicate in the consolidated model also. Then, key work objects and communications are transferred onto the consolidated model for a full view of communication and coordination between roles across the business process.

Figure 4.1 shows the full consolidated flow model for the work practice of energy trading. For this model, we interviewed only salespeople and traders in the energy trading industry. From this data, we uncovered three "unsurfaced" business processes: handling the trades themselves, gathering requirements for the energy needed, and managing the logistics of getting the energy where it's needed. A company could define a composite application to support these processes by just examining this data. Even in the face of new regulations governing energy trading, a model such as this reveals the informal processes already in place that will have to be accounted for in any process redesign.

4.3 Consolidating Sequence Models into the Swim-Lane Diagram

The swim-lane diagram is a method of viewing high-level consolidated sequences to highlight the overall activities in a process and the coordination between the various actors or groups to perform the steps. Each vertical section or "swim lane" represents a person or group; each oval in the chart represents an activity in the process; boxes show the work objects being created and communicated; and annotations show decision points and work objects (see Figure 4.2).

The consolidated swim-lane diagram helps define the functional boundaries of an application by explicitly modeling workflow relationships, internal structure, and work responsibilities. As with the consolidated flow model, the consolidated swim-lane diagram becomes important later as we apply UI building blocks; for example, Guided Procedures may directly represent the steps from this model.

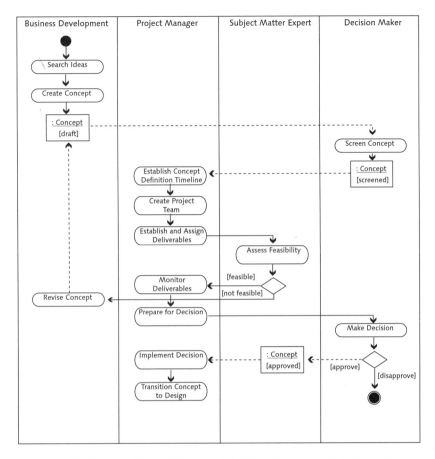

Figure 4.2 The Generate Concept Sequence Workflow from the SAP xPD Project

Individual user sequence models cover a wide range of tasks and mix different levels of detail. Consolidation starts by deciding which sequences are related or are instances of the same procedure and should be represented as part of a larger overall workflow. Sequences covering the same task are collected from several users and compared. Sometimes one sequence precedes another; for example, when the user performs an earlier part of the task first. Sometimes they cover the same actions, but one is more detailed than another. And sometimes they describe alternate strategies for accomplishing the same goal.

Some sequences derived from direct observation may be very detailed. These sequences can be summarized for use in swim-lane diagram consolidation by collecting detailed steps into activities for an initial consolidation. You can set aside the detailed steps for consolidation later, when you want to redesign the particular activity.

Activities are then arranged in order to show how the workflow proceeds. Where the same activity was observed from several users, a single activity is put on the consolidated model. Whenever different users follow different strategies, the consolidated model branches. Where work is handed off between job roles or departments, the activities are put in separate swim lanes to highlight the handoff. The result shows who does the work, what the communication is between people, and what information is consumed, generated, or referenced at each step.

The final step in sequence workflow consolidation is grouping sets of coherent activities into separate *phases*—large groupings of work activities that have meaning to the business. Each phase can be thought of as a unit and managed accordingly. This may not be necessary in cases that deal with smaller business processes, but when a large process is involved, breaking it into phases can help to reveal the structure of the overall process.

This level of sequence consolidation will suffice for most projects when there are preexisting actions or services that can be used to configure the process, so that the detailed work steps don't need to be redesigned. When the process steps required for a sequence break new ground and there's no existing function implemented, the team has to create new designs and implement new actions. This requires a consolidated sequence model that includes the detailed steps within each activity to show the fine structure of the work practice—the strategies and intents that make work organized and efficient. If no detailed sequences cover this task, the team may plan additional short interviews to observe users performing the task. The sequence consolidation is performed in much the same way as described above; more detailed descriptions can be found in the benchmark work on Contextual Design.[1]

---

1 Hugh Beyer and Karen Holtzblatt, *Contextual Design: Defining Customer-Centered Systems*. Morgan Kaufmann Publishers, Inc., San Francisco 1997.

In the SAP xPD project, the overall sequence of developing a new product concept towards implementation was modeled as a high- level sequence model (see Figure 4.3). Across all user interviews, the team collected similar user sequences covering product concept development and design: searching for the initial idea, screening new concepts, assessing feasibility and risk, implementing approved concepts, and so on. The consolidation process produced a *Generate Concept* sequence that represents a common task performed by market research analysts.

Each step within this sequence model represents an activity that can be modeled as a sequence in itself. An example of such a composite activity is the organization of a consumer study. In Chapter 3, we gave an example of such a sequence captured in one interview. This activity was modeled as an individual step within a phase grouping called *Exploring*.

You should note that you can get by with a higher level of detail in your model when choosing from existing UI building blocks, but not when designing new UI screens for actions that aren't supported by the building blocks. New designs depend on the detailed sequence steps of the individual user's task. If the team collects enough detailed data, it can create a consolidated sequence model showing the common pattern and strategies used to accomplish each task that the design will support directly (for more information, refer to the book *Rapid Contextual Design*[2]).

---

2   Karen Holtzblatt, Jessamyn Burns Wendell, Shelley Wood: *Rapid Contextual Design: A How-to Guide to Key Techniques for User-Centered Design*. Morgan Kaufmann Publishers, Inc., San Francisco 2004.

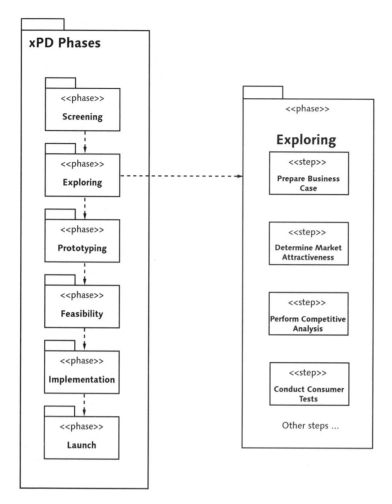

Figure 4.3 Fitting the Phases for the Generate Concept Process into a Business Practice

4.4　Variations in Consolidating Data

4.4.1　Streamlining

A streamlining project puts most of its effort into clarifying the system support for a known process. For such a project, the model consolidation process can be simplified—indeed much of the work can be done by consolidating the design patterns directly, as described above.

An affinity diagram may be a useful way to organize information about users. Often, observation of the work through Contextual Interviews will be mixed with working with a paper prototype. The prototype data leads to a new iteration; the Contextual Interview data is captured as notes and used to build the affinity. This affinity will likely be smaller than one developed by other project types, but it acts as a reminder of the key issues to address, as well as highlighting unknown or hidden issues to the team in advance.

Identifying roles and responsibilities is important for understanding what the system needs to support. The team can start analyzing the roles of one or two key user types to develop a shared set of initial roles. Then interviewers can analyze roles for their own interviews and share their analysis with the rest of the team. By sharing, discussing, and iterating the role identification, the team reaches a shared understanding of the key distinctions. This analysis drives the identification of which UI building blocks to use and how to structure the Activity Centers to support the tasks.

The team may choose to consolidate sequences into swim-lane diagrams. Users may be operating within a work process across people or work groups that need to be understood as a whole and supported directly by the system. In this case, a Guided Procedure is a likely UI building block to use, and a swim-lane diagram can reveal the steps of the procedure. If the team discovers that it needs to build a specific tool for a task, a detailed consolidated sequence model for that task can show the structure that needs to be supported. Otherwise, the sequence consolidation step can be skipped.

4.4.2 Surfacing

A surfacing project deals with poorly understood, implicit processes. More attention to modeling pays dividends for such projects. The basic consolidation described in this chapter is sufficient. Affinity diagrams show the key issues, simple flow consolidations of roles and responsibilities show the needs of individual roles and the core work group, and swim-lane diagrams show the basic process patterns. More complex flow consolidation is necessary only if the data suggests that secondary users must be supported, or a business process must be reinvented. Detailed sequence consolidation can be skipped when existing UI building blocks support the work structure. Simple iteration after the initial construction, based on the data from the interviews, improve these to support the process being surfaced.

A surfacing project expects to introduce work practice and system support for procedures that are currently ad hoc. Therefore, design is guided more by the work intents revealed in the models than by the details of the existing practice. The new system may change procedures and roles, but the original work intent or business goal must not be broken.

4.4.3 Inventing

An inventing project is the most complex and has the highest need for an explicit representation of the work practice. In addition to the activities for a surfacing project, the inventing project benefits from a complete flow consolidation. The flow model should include flow lines and secondary user roles and should be drawn out as a diagram to reveal work interactions. Here, you want to be doing field interviews with the key players in the process. In general, you can expect an inventing project to take longer, demand more resources, and require more interviews to develop a good picture of the work practice being affected.

Unlike streamlining and surfacing projects, the consolidated models in an inventing project drive the team's thinking process. The data is not directly transferred into system design, unless a UI building block is used directly. It is unlikely that UI building blocks will cover the complete new process. Instead, the consolidated data stimulates the team to think of new ways of doing business, the impact that automation can have on productivity, and how the workflow, individual responsibilities, and tasks should be distributed among members of the organization. Consolidation provides the view of the data the team needs, showing them what users are up to and giving the team a visual language to redesign and document the work. Once the team has this data, they can proceed with visioning, storyboarding, and developing the new application.

4.5　UI Building Blocks in Requirements Elicitation

UI building blocks make the design of applications simpler. But they can also simplify the requirements elicitation process by focusing your field interviews, interpretation, and consolidation on just the data that will drive application design. Each of the building blocks depends on certain field data—data about the information to be displayed, the operations to support, and the larger work process to integrate into.

We've already discussed how the building blocks affect the interviewing process. When, in an interview, you recognize that the user's work fits the standard work pattern supported by a building block, you immediately focus on getting the data that the building block needs. A Guided Procedure needs all the steps and actions of the work task, which may have to be collected from several different users. A Work Center needs to collect all the different triggers and monitors that the user refers to, therefore, you must inquire into all the ways the user currently monitors and tracks the work, in addition to tracking frustrations caused by gaps in the ability to monitor.

Data gathering can be simplified further when the interviewer is familiar with the work domain and the building blocks, and when the project is streamlining in nature—it is supporting the work without changing it in major ways. First, conduct a small number of field interviews to validate your initial understanding—just as you would before building a prototype—and use these interviews to instantiate your initial set of building blocks. Then, you can use the building blocks directly in the interview, capturing requirements either as properties of the building block or by sketching the UI itself.

For example, you might identify a coherent set of responsibilities supporting one of the user's roles and believe it to be a good starting point for a Work Center. You would then start laying out a Work Center with the user—sketching the screen, mapping each responsibility to a function in the Work Center, adding monitors and triggers as appropriate, and adding contextual views and actions to the contextual navigation panel to support related work. Each view and action can be described in more detail to capture purpose, sequence information, and other insights. The user's involvement makes your sketch more complete and gives you immediate feedback on whether you've understood this job role correctly. You can start with your initial understanding and change it accordingly, in response to the user's input. This is a standard mock-up interview as described in Chapter 7.

You interpret the interview in the same way as you would a paper prototyping session. During the interview, you discover new aspects of work practice, you capture specific design ideas in your preliminary building block sketches, and your conversation with the user has sparked issues and design ideas. In the interpretation session, you walk through the interview separating out these different kinds of data, resulting in a deeper understanding of the work practice and detailed feedback on your ideas for using the building blocks.

Once you've done this with several users, you can build an affinity diagram to see the issues and revise the building blocks to address problems and incorporate good ideas. The design changes are usually limited to step-by-step, incremental changes over your preliminary ideas and the current work practice. You may choose to run visioning sessions to look for more significant changes that can potentially offer more significant improvements to the work process.

5 Designing with Building Blocks

Up to this point, we've been discussing the recommended process for requirements gathering and analysis. The next step is designing the system functionality, behavior, and user interface to meet the requirements.

This design comes from matching requirements to the capabilities of your frontend and the available UI building blocks provided by the development platform. When we talk about building blocks, we mean packaged templates combining both user interface and behavior, designed to organize and support a work task. Many tasks are similar in structure and can be supported by the same UI building block—the data manipulated and function names are different, but the structure of the UI is the same. When using such building blocks, application designers can focus on the design of the task-specific UI and content, instead of struggling with basic navigational design questions.

Depending on the existence of such building blocks and the appropriateness of applying them to requirements defined in the work models, this effort can either be very streamlined, by applying principles and mapping rules, or it may be time-consuming, requiring good design skills.

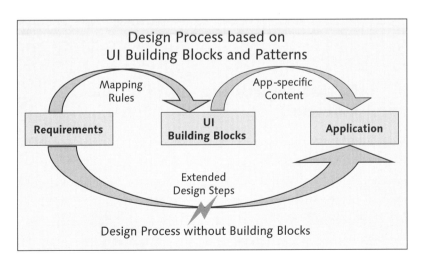

Figure 5.1 Design with and without Building Blocks

The challenge for a business platform is to find the right balance between predefined building blocks and the flexibility to optimize the design of one particular composite application. Requirements for some applications are very task- or domain-specific and cannot be applied to other solutions.

However, many design aspects of business applications are recurring and can be generalized into reusable building blocks. For example, you will most likely find the following usage scenarios in any business application:

▶ Users have role-based access to business functions.

▶ They create and edit instances of business objects.

▶ They participate in a business workflow and follow procedures.

▶ They are interested in analytics that display the status of the business.

▶ Collaboration and coordination activities are both informal and formal.

To make this chapter applicable to any composite application, we want to focus on such common design challenges rather than on the detailed UI design of a task-specific user-interaction design. Therefore, we'll introduce an information architecture of business applications with its implied building blocks and elements like roles, tasks, and context.

5.1 Information Architecture of Business Applications

Laying out all functions and information of a new business application across several screens is always a challenge. It feels like flattening an n-dimensional problem space into a two-dimensional screen design. The number of ways to cluster content into a sequential navigation can become overwhelming quickly. Often, there is not adequate screen real estate to put all the functions on the same screen. Even a well-designed and consistent navigational structure can result in white space on the screen and put important functions too many clicks away from the entry screen.

Design is the process of transforming a set of requirements identified in the work models into a design constrained by physical and technical limitations of the system. Because there is not much guidance for this process, many designs are based on the intuition of user-interaction designers and undocumented best practices of application design.

In Contextual Design, the design phase is supported by the User Environment Design model as a formal method of getting to an abstract description of an application structure by considering some principles and heuristics of mapping task flows to screen layouts. The User Environment Design model introduces *focus areas* that support all functions necessary to enable the user to accomplish a coherent set of tasks that hang together by a common work intent. A focus area typically maps to a page or subarea of a screen. Application design becomes a matter of identifying focus areas, filling them with content, and linking them to related focus areas.

To speed up this process, the SAP NetWeaver platform introduces an information architecture tailored for business applications by providing standard navigational structures and building blocks, which are predefined focus areas. The goal of the SAP NetWeaver platform is to accelerate the design process by providing ready-to-use UI building blocks and accelerators in the form of templates or predefined basic navigation behaviors that can be mapped to the specific requirements of the new application.

You can think of such predefined information architecture for applications as a kind of Contextual Design User Environment that comes with basic focus areas, and guidance on how to fill and extend them based on the requirements of your new application. So the first question for design is "Is there a predefined focus area or building block that provides the right structure to support a task?"

Through field interviews and model consolidation, you understand your users' work requirements and the overall process, functions, and collaboration required to support that work. If you also understand that building blocks are available to can identify the set of building blocks that you can use to support this work and the way to populate each building block with role-specific or process-specific content and services.

This process of mapping data to building blocks significantly speeds up your development process. Instead of designing each part of the system uniquely, you construct a new system by configuring building blocks. Where a building block exists, it needs to be fleshed out with the specific data and function for the application. Where no building block exists, new UI components need to be designed and integrated into the application, driven by the more detailed work requirements you have collected in the field.

Having a standard information architecture in place is a best practice for information websites or shopping sites. This chapter describes how a business platform like SAP NetWeaver provides a similar approach for business applications. The proposed information architecture is driven by the following key principles:

▶ **Work Zooming**
We assume that users start from a general orientation and planning level and incrementally focus on a specific business context or business actions.

▶ **Contextual Work**
We assume that work is often done in a discrete work context or work situation in which a user is performing one or more actions.

5.1.1 Work Zooming

Part of the job is to design a navigation framework that puts the user in control—letting users drive the interface following their own work intents, instead of being driven by the structure of database tables or other implementation models.

At a high level, users want to get an overall view of their work before diving into a particular task. Users need to see what's happening, where the major issues are, and what deadlines are looming; they can focus first on a specific part of their job and then start work on a specific task. The navigation framework should support the practice of work zooming.

Each layer supports a different level of work zooming—looking across the whole job, focusing on an area of concern, or working on a specific task. Each layer comes with its building blocks that provide a structure for supporting work at that level (see Figure 5.2).

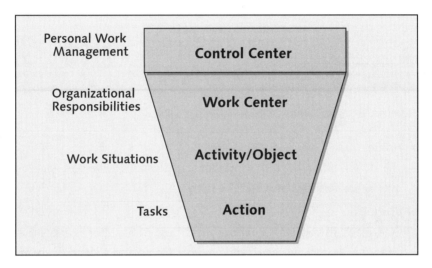

Figure 5.2 Work Zooming and Related UI Building Blocks

The Control Center monitors and plans personal work

At this level, users have an overview of their work where they can track ongoing work and accept triggers for new work. Users generally perform multiple roles, and the Control Center shows a user all the key tasks (or all tasks he or she is tracking) across all roles. This level provides a coherent view of a person's job. Users can decide what to do next without focusing on a particular role or work task.

The Control Center consists of distinct places with each one providing different aspects of user productivity, as illustrated in Figure 5.3. At the Control Center level, all information displayed is aggregated across all activities.

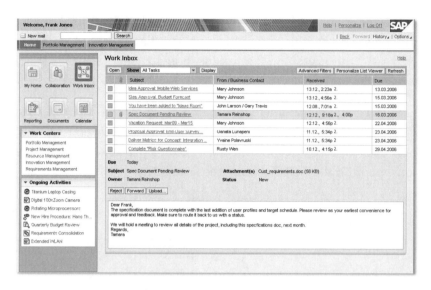

Figure 5.3 A Sample Control Center with New Work Items

▶ **Home**

The default login page that provides a newspaper-like personalized overview showing the work of a user.

▶ **Work list**

One place to receive workflow messages, notifications, and other messages that trigger new work; a work list should give an overview about the workload originating from standard piles of work.

▶ **Work schedule**

Business-related time management.

▶ **Business monitor**

One place to track the status of business a user is responsible for or interested in; a business monitor should provide condensed status watch lists of the most essential business entities, as well as collections of reports for monitoring business key performance indicators (KPIs).

▶ **Activities**

A list of all ad-hoc activities that are initiated, owned, or supervised by the user; a place for all tasks that require a long-running effort to be accomplished and may include collaboration with others.

As you can see, the structure of the control-center level is influenced solely by the requirement to support individual users to coordinate and plan work, and not by the business logic or database records. The optimization of user productivity drives most of the design of the Control Center.

5.1.2 Contextual Work

Another key principle is to design a business application to reflect the work intent and focus of users. Most workers do not change work context with every observable action. Without being aware of it, users perform tasks in the context of some work situation. The SAP xApp Product Definition (SAP xPD) product manager may sign a contract in the context of a new-hire process, or he may assess the market potential in the context of a new-product introduction project. There is always some work context around the actual task performed by people.

Some workers may be highly reactive in their work, responding to any triggered request that appears. However, for most business workers, several actions tend to hang together by a common work goal or work situation. It is those context clusters that you have to identify in order to structure your business applications into coherent chunks of functionality that truly support the user's intent and action.

Once users have an overview of their work in the Control Center and have decided what to do next, they start to focus on a particular task. Those tasks can be short-term activities that require a small amount of contextual information to accomplish, or they may be ongoing activities that take place over time and require collaboration with others. These longer, potentially collaborative tasks may themselves be composed of tasks that need context.

Context-oriented building blocks help you to sort requirements into a navigational structure that embodies the necessary information and action to support the activity in one place. In Contextual Design terminology, building blocks provide you with clear guidance regarding what focus areas to define and what related functions to include. When context-oriented building blocks are provided by business platforms such as SAP NetWeaver, composite-application projects can quickly lay out the application structure. Now, we'll describe some of the types of building blocks that we have designed.

Work Centers for zooming on job responsibilities

In the Work Center, the user focuses on a specific subset of his or her organizational job role. A Work Center contains all functions and content necessary for one overarching job responsibility—usually all the work associated with a single role as defined in the consolidated role model.

Work Centers are the top-level navigational building blocks of a composite application and are hooked into the activities list of the Control Center as navigational entry points. SAP xApps ship with one or more Work Centers, depending on how many roles and job functions are supported.

Work Centers are robust work packages that can be assigned to different jobs in different combinations. For example, in the SAP xPD composite application, the product manager has a Work Center for managing and tracking product requirements. This Work Center is appropriate not only for product managers, but for anyone who is responsible for managing new requirements, independent of their job title.

Work Centers typically support a role as defined by your consolidated data; sometimes a set of closely-related roles will be supported by a single Work Center. They bundle a coherent set of functions to support work intents related to the role. The functions should be exhaustive enough that the user needn't switch Work Centers within one task flow. This may result in some redundancy between the Control Center and a Work Center or two Work Centers, but the user's work will flow better when there is some duplicated function rather than when the user must go searching through the interface for a needed function.

Figure 5.4 shows the rendered UI for a Work Center for product Innovation Management. Key views and actions are in the contextual panel on the left, with an overview of the work (in this case the ongoing product concept the manager is currently involved in) on the right.

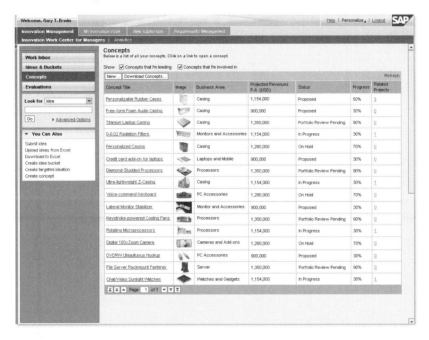

Figure 5.4 A Work Center for Product Innovation

The contextual panel on the left contains standard contextual views and actions links for controlling the interface and accessing work objects within a given work context. Each of these navigational elements is defined to support a task or action the user might want to perform while doing work in the context of this role. These tasks can be defined directly from the consolidated role model, which defines roles and responsibilities that must be supported by the Work Center.

The right pane changes depending on the link selected on the left. It provides the place to display the UI of the selected service. The details of this pane are designed to support a single task, as defined by a consolidated sequence model or as listed as a responsibility in the role definition.

Ad-Hoc Activity Centers for zooming on work situations

An Activity Center contains all functions and content necessary for one specific work situation. For example, the product manager may work on one specific product concept by launching an Activity Center that holds together all related information and provides some related actions meaningful for this activity. While working within the Activity Center, the product manager may, for example, request information from experts regarding their assessment of proposed new product features and store all the assessments within this Activity Center.

The interaction design of Work Centers and Activities Centers is very similar, however, the underlying requirements are different. An Activity Center is zooming in on an instance of a long-running task and helps to pull together all functions and artifacts involved in a particular work situation. For example, it contains all the accumulated work associated with a specific project or all information related to the resolution of a complex problem. In contrast, a Work Center is not focused on one particular task, but on a set of general responsibilities implied by an organizational work role. Work Centers bundle work and ongoing tasks related to a long-term organizational job role.

Whenever a task requires more than just a short-term interaction with an application, an Activity Center can be used so the task context and the corresponding activities can persist, thereby helping the user to accomplish this task.

Such tasks may reflect work situations or processes with varying degrees of complexity:

▶ **Personal Versus Collaborative**
A task may be handled as a personal, standalone task, or may expand to a collaborative workflow.

▶ **Procedural Versus Ad Hoc**
Some tasks have best practices associated with them that recommend how to accomplish them. In such cases, the application can provide procedural guidance that leads the user through the necessary steps or recommends the best-practice choice of action. For

example, the activity of evaluating a new product idea can be presented as standardized procedures that require assessments from R&D, marketing, legal, and packaging.

▶ **Simple Versus Composite**

Some tasks can be accomplished in one step, while other tasks require multiple actions or subactivities to be completed. For example, submitting an idea can be a rather simple activity that requires only one action, while driving a new product concept through to production is a very complex task composed of many actions and subactivities.

If an action is simple and can be done in just one or two actions, it is not perceived by the user as a separate activity. Instead, it is an action performed within the context in which the user is currently working. Later, we will show design examples for such *contextual actions*, that is, actions that appear within the current context and can be completed by the user without switching to a new context. Actions become complex if user knowledge is not sufficient to execute the activity immediately, or if the nature of the work situation requires that one or several users must perform multiple actions.

With regard to the work models described earlier in this book, the sequence model is key to understanding concrete work situations. Any important activity should be modeled by a sequence model. The number of steps within a sequence provides insights about the complexity of the activity and the degree of collaboration required to accomplish the business goal.

Depending on the complexity of a sequence, it may or may not be appropriate to model the task as an Activity Center. If workflow steps are pushed to users, it may suffice to design *quick actions*, focusing on just the task execution and not so much on the context. Quick actions let the user choose from a limited set of options, or prompt the user for data required by the workflow. Quick actions are often just smaller steps within a larger sequence model, or a swim-lane diagram prompting the user to decide which option to choose or to enter data without displaying the entire context of the underlying process context. They are the tip of the iceberg, which, in this case, would be the entire work-flow context. Designers have to decide how much a user needs to see of this iceberg when making decisions. For example, a simple approval of a leave request typically requires only a single-screen interactive message and not a complex Activity Center.

Since an approval comes and goes quickly, the user does not need a continual independent activity. Depending on the complexity of the task as it is performed by a particular role, a quick action may bring more or less information. For example, ranking a new product idea according to its innovation level might be a simple task if the user is an expert, but it may expand to collaborative tasks if the new product idea is more complex and requires evaluations from several experts.

The design of Activity Centers may be driven by entire sequence models or swim-lane diagrams; however, the design may correspond to a long-running task that does not have an established sequence but is, instead, a set of options from among which a user can choose. In Con-textual Interviews, such tasks will be captured as a responsibility in interviews and not as a sequence, because there is no clear order implied by best practices.

For all activities that cannot be handled by a single focused action, there is an opportunity to recommend a certain order of performing multiple actions within the given work situation that is implied by business rules or informal best practices For this type of work context, the SAP NetWeaver platform provides Guided Procedures, an interactive dynamic workflow interface to drive collaborative processes.

When a preconfigured process drives the user's actions, the Guided Procedure's UI walks the user through the process step by step. Guided Procedures support collaboration among multiple users all working towards a common goal, each contributing their share. UI elements of the Guided Procedure allow for navigation through the process, indicate the status of the process, and provide different views on the process.

Guided Procedures support the introduction of phases that are divided into steps. Such steps and phases of a Guided Procedure may come directly from the consolidated swim-lane diagram.

Many people might contribute to complete a process in an organization, so different steps and phases of a Guided Procedure may be completed by different people. The Guided Procedure tracks handoff and coordination among people and provides interfaces to support doing the work.

In Figure 5.5, the UI design for a Guided Procedure, which is implementing the sequence model of developing one product concept, is shown. The larger phases are displayed as a roadmap across the top of the screen; the left-hand contextual panel shows the activities to be performed in this phase. The main body of the interface shows a simple action for one activity in the process.

Figure 5.5 A Guided Procedure Step within the Product Innovation Process

Guided Procedures provide users with focused contexts that contain appropriate information and actions for each level of work. When users are at the highest level, they have an overview of the work; however, when they are at a detailed step, they can focus on a single action.

Users cannot successfully focus on multiple levels simultaneously. The SAP NetWeaver building-block design enables users to zoom into a specific level to do work and then to zoom out (or back out) to reestablish their understanding of the entire process.

Object instance views for zooming on business objects

Business objects are another prominent context for focused work that's supported by SAP NetWeaver building blocks. Sometimes users have to focus on a single business object; for example, to create or modify a single product requirement that is managed in the SAP xPD application, or to evaluate one specific new product idea. Such an object-centric focus area combines appropriate information presentation of the object with the tools required to perform all necessary actions. A business object in SAP xPD might be, for example, a specific product or a single requirement.

For example, in Figure 5.6, an object instance view for a single product concept is shown. The left-hand contextual panel lists actions that are meaningful in the context of product concepts. The phase indicator reminds the user that there is also a development roadmap for such projects. As you can see, object context and activity context can sometimes converge to form one integrated design.

What information of the business object is appropriate to display depends on the work situation. A generic object view may not be sufficient. Depending on the work and process role, different perspectives (views) on the concrete instance of the business object are required to inform the user what to do next. For example, if a product manager wants to update a single product requirement, all information about the requirement, such as the change history of this requirement and information about relationships to other requirements, should be available.

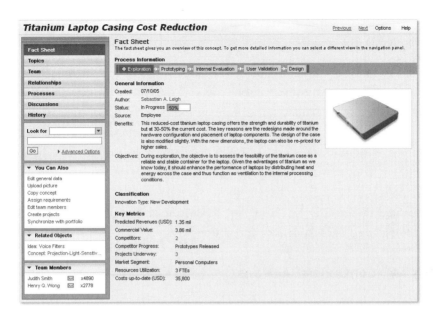

Figure 5.6 An Object Instance View Showing the Facts of One Concept at-a-Glance

We call this UI building block the object instance view, because it provides views and related actions for one object instance. The idea is to provide an at-a-glance view of the status and basic information of a selected object, as well as access to appropriate related actions. Object-centered views make sense when the main focus of the work is to manage this object—to develop the product concept, manage the requirement, specify a product feature, and so on.

However, if your design is well informed by work models that make the user intent transparent and explicit, then the content in the object instance view will be influenced mainly by the context of the activity and not by the object. For example, when a marketing person works on a requirements structure for a new product release, he or she considers high-level marketing requirements and may want to break down requirements into more specific success measures. In contrast, a technical person may be tasked to create the exact specifications. This person focuses on the detailed target values and wants to understand the technical options and relationships. So, even though both roles are looking at the same requirements structure, the work intents and, consequently, the required information and tools are very different.

Be careful when designing object instance views; focus on the activity and not the object instance itself. You may even discover that an Activity Center or a Guided Procedure is more suitable to support the underlying work intent than a generic object instance view. Generic object instance views are usually a backup design for use cases you haven't considered or don't have the necessary resources to currently handle. As soon as you have a good understanding of the activity performed by the user, you can start to customize the building block by adding specific perspectives and actions.

5.1.3 Contextual Actions

Actions are the atomic tasks that users perform in a given work context or activity. These tasks can comprise a step users execute within the context of a procedural activity or an action they take within any of the other activity building blocks. If an action is simple and well-defined, a user expects to launch the action within the current context. For example, when a product manager is working on a collection of requirements for a new release, he or she may need to update the status of one of the requirements. The manager performs a single action within the current context, instead of opening the requirement and losing focus on the whole collection.

The detailed UI design of the action itself is determined by the task that is executed, but the general appearance should be consistent. Depending on the complexity of interaction, one action may correspond to exactly one screen, or several screens may divide the interaction into steps or coherent clusters of input fields.

▶ **Simple Actions**
Such actions are supported by a single screen that can be launched within a context next to the contextual panel. For example, submitting an idea could be an action offered in the context of an SAP xPD Work Center for managing requirements (see Figure 5.7).

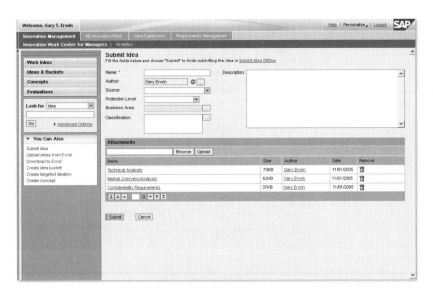

Figure 5.7 A Simple Action Providing Quick Entry within the Context of a Work Center

▶ **Guided Actions**

Such actions require a multiple-screen sequence that models the task or interaction flow needed to perform this action. Unlike a Guided Procedure, which represents a context in itself and covers the entire screen, the scope of a guided action is limited to a transient personal task flow within a larger context, or to a wizard-like sequence limited by the constraints of screen real estate or designed to assist untrained users.

In Figure 5.8, you see an example of guided actions for creating a product concept. Since there are many steps to perform, the action is divided into several steps in order to avoid overloaded screens and to better aid the product manager.

If there is the need for persistence, and each step can be assigned to different users, the Guided Procedures building block is more appropriate.

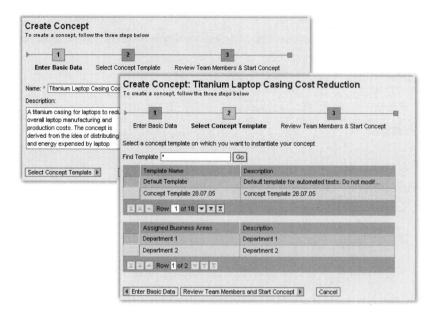

Figure 5.8 A Guided Action for Creating a Product Concept in the System

SAP NetWeaver building blocks provide the necessary components to design an architecture for many standard business processes. Using just these components, you can create overviews, focused Activity Centers, Guided Procedures, detailed tasks, and steps within tasks. These generic components help you with getting a quick start on building your application. Just fill in the data and you'll have a prototype ready to test and iterate with users.

In the next section, we discuss how to map the user data you collected into these building blocks.

5.2 Mapping Consolidated Requirements into Building Blocks

In any business application design, tension exists between process-centered requirements (what the process needs to serve the business) and user-centered requirements (what the user would prefer if all that mattered was getting the job done). The requirements are often collected by different experts (business engineers or solution architects versus ethnographic engineers or user experience specialists) and are usually captured as disconnected requirement documents. How do we merge these two perspectives into one coherent picture that helps us to map individual task flow to company processes?

A composite application should increase both user productivity and business efficiency. People run the enterprise and the processes in it. Conversely, any activity that a person does in an organization is related to a larger process in one way or another. Understanding these relationships enables us to design systems that support the process requirements appropriately without interfering with the user's work focus.

Users are acting within actual work situations, each of which defines a specific work context. Depending on the task, this context can be limited to the individual task, or span the entire underlying process. A simple approval request for an absence of an employee usually requires only limited information for the decision maker. An approval of a new acquisition may, alternatively, require a complete understanding of the assessments being made as prerequisites to making a decision. To support work practice, we must understand what the current work context is, as well as the scope for users, when they interact with the system and what information needs result from these interactions.

In this section, we focus on work context from two complementing perspectives on corporate work support. The first perspective is how to identify and support roles defined by the organization or within a concrete process instance; the second perspective is how to support the accomplishment of tasks that support responsibilities defined by these roles. We introduce the concept of context maps as a generic way to translate such role- or task-based requirements into context descriptions that drive the structure of a new composite application.

5.2.1 Supporting Roles

One way of beginning to map requirements to application design is to start from your role list, focusing on the most central roles for the business scenario that you want to support. Review your flow model or role list and ask yourself what kind of roles you have:

▶ *Work roles* are natural bundles of responsibilities that evolve out of everyday practices. They reflect how work is clustered into organizational work packages that hang together by common work intent or business goals and can be executed by one person. The focus of a work role is on doing some specific work on a continuous basis. This can be knowledge work that is not directly related to any tangible business process, such as developing a new marketing strategy or inventing new products. It can be so high level that the direct connection to a process is not relevant. For example, a vice president of development is not deeply involved in one particular product development. Instead, she manages the resources and timelines across all development projects. She is busy with setting directions, managing the portfolio, and aggregating data for consolidated reports and planning. In a more workflow-oriented work role, the role may be assigned permanently to a system workflow step, such as entering data, reviewing travel expenses, booking trips, receiving returns, or dispatching problem messages. Although those workers are performing one step within a larger business process, the permanent assignment to this step makes it feel like a standalone responsibility. These employees develop their special work practice of processing piles of work items in an efficient way.

▶ *Ad-hoc process roles* are roles that exist only in the context of one process or work situation, and describe the responsibilities in the context of that instance. A user is responsible for a process role only when a specific activity is instantiated. For example, when a manager promotes an employee, the manager and employee each take on specific roles in that particular promotion process. The manager is the requester (initiator); the employee is the object being promoted. An HR agent may act as an advisor and facilitator, possibly as the process driver as well. The boss of the manager is the approver. All the players are interested in monitoring the completion of the process until it is done. After that, they are no longer interested, and the process instance itself no longer exists, or will be archived. The same user can play different roles in different instances of the same process pattern For example, depending on who gets promoted, a manager can be the approver, the requester, or the person being promoted.

Don't forget that ultimately, real people are doing the work—all workers playing multiple roles in multiple process instances. Work roles represent continuous responsibilities that a user is responsible for at any time.

Each person is responsible for a combination of work roles and the application that workers use must support the whole job. Plan for their initial entry point—the Control Center—to give them a quick overview of all their roles; Work Centers to give them a coherent place to initiate and monitor activities; and Activity Centers to help them manage and execute their long-running tasks.

Here's an example of working from data to design for SAP xPD, the project we've been following throughout this book.

For the SAP xPD project, we have the following roles:

Role Name	Role Description	Responsibility
Innovation Driver (U3, U9, U5)	Person who drives the generation of ideas	▶ Leads innovation projects (U3) ▶ Works with advanced technology groups (U3) ▶ Guides product exploration and development teams (U9) ▶ Schedules brainstorm session with task forces (U9) ▶ Scans preexisting insights (U9) ▶ Collects ideas for consideration as potential new concepts (U9) ▶ Generates proposals for new ideas (U9)

Table 5.1 Examples of SAP xPD Work Roles

Role Name	Role Description	Responsibility
		▶ Classifies ideas (U5)
		▶ Submits ideas to idea portal (U5)
		▶ Analyzes consumer data (U5)
Concept Introduction Shepherd (U9, U5, U6)	Person who ensures that ideas generated by advanced technology (or other) groups are properly introduced into the product definition system	▶ Tracks ongoing work in other groups that may become potential concepts (U9, U5)
		▶ Identifies responsible leaders in other groups to handle the introduction (U5)
		▶ Tracks and reminds people in other groups about the process and deadlines (U9, U6)
		▶ Provides notification and rewards to teams when their prototypes pass milestones in the product definition process (U6)

Table 5.1 Examples of SAP xPD Work Roles (cont.)

The *Innovation Driver* is an example of a general work role; in this role, the user generates new ideas and concepts for introduction to the product definition system. One of the responsibilities is to lead innovation projects. Leading a specific project is a process role that probably includes being the owner or driver of a selected innovation project. This implies tracking the progress and performing ad-hoc coordination tasks related to this project. As soon as the project is done, this responsibility ends.

The *Concept Introduction Shepherd* is also a work role. In this role, the user oversees processes in which others are doing the real work. He or she acts as a policy and best-practice watcher and needs corresponding tools to manage the portfolio of all product concept projects and to track quality metrics. The person in this role is not participating in the day-to-day work; his or her activities are not part of the process. Instead, this person is an informal overseer, a role that evolved over time by best practices.

Work roles

Supporting a work role will likely require a Work Center. This Work Center collects key performance indicators (KPIs), functions, and views that support the work of the role, all of which are revealed by the role's responsibilities. For the innovation driver's Work Center, we could define the following views:

▶ An *overview* shows all the work associated with a work role. This view is a newspaper-like summary page. It contains—in one condensed view—the gist of the activities the user is currently focusing on within one particular role. The overview aggregates data from all subactivities, especially information about new messages, exceptions, and work status. For an innovation driver, this overview should include monitoring components to display the status of the user's different innovation projects, any scheduled brainstorming sessions, an indication of proposals and ideas that need to be worked on, and overall KPIs, such as how many product-definition concepts are currently in the pipeline and their current success rate. For SAP xPD, this implies that the Work Center should include summaries of outstanding concepts and ideas and their status and KPIs showing such measures as how many concepts make it to product stage and how many concepts are introduced per month.

▶ A *message* (*What's New*) view is appropriate when a work role includes the processing of alerts, exceptions, or notifications that are produced by workflow or the system and which the user has to acknowledge and react to. In SAP xPD, these include notifications that a concept has progressed from one stage to the next, that a deadline has passed with no action on a concept, and that approval on a concept is needed from the user. The message view acts as a filtered subset of message types that can also be seen in the inbox of the Control Center.

▶ A *work list* view is appropriate when a work role includes the processing of work items—not generic exceptions or unpredictable messages, but activity-specific work items produced by workflow or by the system and which the user must process on a daily basis. For example, new internal purchase order requests are typical work items for a purchaser. If they come in on a regular basis and represent a core work list for this role, the work list warrants its own view. In SAP xPD, the innovation driver would want new ideas to show up in the work list for evaluation and introduction as concepts.

▶ An *ongoing work-tracking* view uses table-like dashboards to list KPIs of ongoing activities and business objects that are essential to a user. The dashboard functions as a "business watch list" and provides a convenient way of monitoring the work status and navigating to the actual work instance. The innovation driver should have dashboards showing the concepts that he or she is monitoring; the concept introduction shepherd could benefit from tracking emerging ideas in the pre-concept stage to ensure they make it into the product definition process.

Finally, work often focuses on important business objects related to the role. These business objects are often named in the role's responsibilities and can be identified in the swim-lane diagram. For the innovation driver, ideas and concepts are central objects that the role needs to manipulate. These objects should be listed in the object lookup section of the contextual panel for quick search and browsing.

Process roles

Process roles describe how people participate or contribute to specific processes. While work roles represent permanent work assignments defined by the company, the lifetime of a process role is linked to the process step or work situation. For example, a user of the SAP xPD application can participate in multiple innovation projects but have different roles for each project. In one project, the user could be the project owner; in another, a contributor. Process roles require various types of system support, depending on what the role is about. Typical process roles include the following displayed in Figure 5.9:

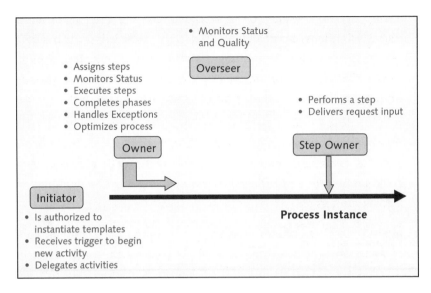

Figure 5.9 Standard Process Roles

▶ The *Process Initiator* is the role that starts a process. Since people start processes as part of their ongoing responsibility originating from a work role, the Work Center should provide functionality to start such processes. For example, when scanning a new product idea, a product manager may initiate the assessment of this idea by starting a new product concept project. The manager does not do the work; instead, he or she delegates the work to a team member who is responsible for ensuring that the assessment is completed.

▶ The *Process Owner* is responsible for a process with respect to quality of outcome and accomplishments. A process driver watches the process because he or she cares about the progress. As a driver, the user of the SAP xPD application sends reminders, invites contributors, and assigns tasks. This person works primarily within the Guided Procedure building block of SAP NetWeaver, which provides an overview of the process with all the necessary management functions.

▶ The *Process Step Owner* role is responsible for performing one step of a larger process. The step owner receives work items that carry all the information necessary to execute the step. Depending on the complexity of the step, this information can be limited to a simple yes/no decision screen, or it may point to the original business object or process context. This may map to different UI building blocks, such as quick action, object instance view, or Activity Center. As participants in the process, step owners need to have tasks and exceptions show up in their inbox or work list views in order to process them.

▶ The *Process Overseer* role tracks the progress of an ongoing process instance. Overseers need an at-a-glance overview of a process. This could be in form of KPI dashboards displaying ongoing work within a Work Center.

In addition to these process-specific roles, some organizational work roles focus on processes, but as a whole (see Figure 5.10). Users in these roles are not actors in a particular process instance, but oversee all instances of a certain type. They are tasked to monitor or oversee a process without being involved in any particular instance. Interfaces for them focus less on the content of one process instance and more on the portfolio and quality of the process itself. Those jobs map to work roles because the responsibilities are ongoing and not linked to a particular process instance.

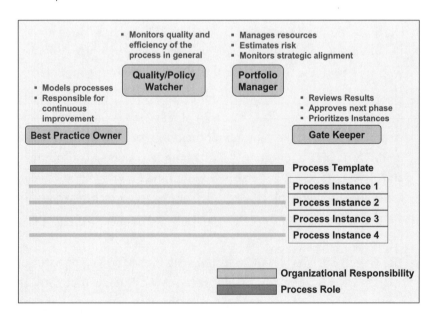

Figure 5.10 Organizational Work Roles Focusing on Processes in General

▶ The *Best-Practice Owner* is responsible for the design and continuous improvement of a process. This is an organizational work role related to process efficiency. The best-practice owner owns one or many process templates and receives requests for modifications in his or her inbox. Creating and modifying workflow templates are core actions. Contextual views in this Work Center provide performance metrics and support monitoring of performance of each template. This role also enforces other people to follow best practices.

▶ The *Quality/Policy Watcher* is responsible for the compliance and quality of instances of processes. Information needs are very similar to the Best-Practice Owners, except that violations of business rules and quality of outcome is more important than the efficiency of KPIs.

▶ The *Portfolio Manager* looks across all instances of one or several items to monitor strategic alignment of company activities or to forecast resource demands based on planned projects. Sometimes the portfolio manager acts as a process overseer, monitoring the as-is status from a high-level perspective. These users need aggregated information and statistics as well as simple ways to maintain and monitor their portfolio.

▶ The *Gate Keeper* is authorized to approve or reject the transition of a process from one phase into the next phase. For example, innovation projects may transition from the exploration phase to the substantiation phase only after a formal stage/gate step that reviews the project and approves the next phase. These roles need to be enabled to efficiently review the project history and intermediate results.

Considering this list of roles, it is likely that the innovation driver plays the process owner role in several innovation projects. The driver can also be a process step owner in projects for which he or she is not directly responsible. The process role is always defined in the context of one particular project.

The concept introduction shepherd exists to feed the product definition process—to ensure that researchers who would much rather be exploring new ideas get their work properly documented and entered into the product definition system. This job is clearly that of a process overseer. In this role, the user ensures that specific ideas are properly entered into the product definition system and makes certain that others perform their process responsibilities. This responsibility is not tightly associated with one particular instance (project) and can therefore be modeled as a work role supported by a Work Center.

When surfacing a process that does not currently have explicit support, we invent a new role, the process overseer, because the process that has been surfaced needs someone to make sure the process is followed. A process that is already a standard part of the way the organization does business might lack an explicit process overseer role and could now benefit from one to improve process efficiency.

Consider how best-practice owner or process overseer roles are useful for the processes you're introducing in your composite application. This provides a way to go beyond the standard ERP paradigm by introducing a focus on measuring and monitoring the process, thereby encouraging continuous process improvement.

5.2.2 Supporting Tasks

Tasks are like the tip of an iceberg. Tasks are most often just a small piece within a much larger context. When interpreting Contextual Interviews try to look "under the water" and estimate what is under and behind the task you have just observed. Any task you observe points you to a larger context, such as a potential work role or process you might want to support.

Tasks are typically embedded in one of the following contexts:

▶ **Tasks as Part of a Work Role**
Contextual tasks that relate to one work role, but not to one particular object or process instance, map to an action performed in the context of a Work Center. Supporting functions should be put in the *You Can* section of the contextual panel.

▶ **Tasks as Part of Manipulating Objects**

Tasks that directly affect work objects, and cannot be executed without having one or more objects selected, map to an object service embedded in an object-centered work instance view in order to manipulate a particular object.

▶ **Tasks as Part of a Larger Activity**

Tasks embedded in a larger work procedure map to a step within a Guided Procedure template, or a *You Can* action within an Activity Center.

▶ **Tasks as Responses to a Work Item**

Tasks are often delivered as a work item. A work item is typically assigned to the user and carries enough information to respond or point to the original context that created this work item. This context is typically a system workflow, a collaborative procedure, or an ad-hoc request originating from activities that other users accomplish as part of their responsibilities. These tasks are delivered in Work Centers as role-specific work lists or pushed as a request into a universal inbox.

Tasks may differ significantly with respect to their internal complexity and lifetime. Tasks might map to simple transient actions requiring a single screen or a sequence of screens. They may also map to long-running activities creating an entire new work context like a subprocess or an ad-hoc activity. From the perspective of the parent context, they are launched as one single step that is either transient or long-running.

Depending on the complexity, tasks require different technical constructs in the business platform:

▶ **Simple Task—Single Screens**

A simple task can be accomplished by a single action and typically requires only one screen for data entry. The design of this screen is determined by the detailed consolidated sequence model for the task and by any work objects manipulated in performing the task. There is no general design pattern for this screen.

▶ **Simple Task—Multiple Screens**

Some tasks, though conceptually simple, require more user interaction than can a single screen can accommodate. These tasks can be split across multiple screens using the consolidated sequence model to identify natural break points. They are still perceived as a single action, however, the system guides the user through a series of screens.

▶ **Long-Running Activities**

A complex task often persists over some amount of time and may include collaboration with other actors. Those activities represent a larger procedure, such as the exploration of a new product concept. It may require status tracking or the involvement of multiple contributors. The steps within the activity are best supported by steps within a Guided Procedure. An overall swim-lane diagram defines the structure of the Guided Procedure, and consolidated sequence models define the structure of individual task steps. If there is no natural or logical sequence, they are best modeled as Activity Centers that bundle all necessary content and functions just like Work Centers do for work roles.

Tasks enable users to discharge their responsibilities—the responsibilities that are either part of a work role or a process role. Sometimes such responsibilities feel like a separate work role, because an entire set of coherent tasks are involved and have to be supported. Sometimes they correspond to a limited set of tasks that require special functions that feel like a special tool. In such cases, tasks can map to one of the following building blocks:

▶ **Secondary Work Center**

A complex responsibility is similar to a small work role; all the tasks are oriented towards accomplishing that responsibility. The tasks may consist of more than one step requiring inspection, thinking, writing, and other activities. For a complex task with multiple steps, you might use a secondary Work Center that can be launched as an action from within a primary Work Center.

▶ **Activity Center**

If a responsibility is accomplished by initiating long-running activities, like projects or task forces, the information and functions necessary to accomplish the task should be modeled as activities with their own building blocks such as ad-hoc Guided Procedures or object instance views.

▶ **Complex Tool**

A task may require the launching of a specialized application that offers all the functions to accomplish the task. For example, the task "develop organizational structure" requires an organization chart builder that is launched and used for a significant period of time. Often these applications are legacy systems or specialized ERP applications. In such cases, the parent context design treats the specialized application as a single action, providing convenient flow to and from the application, and perhaps making its work objects available for sharing in other building blocks, but not changing the specialized application itself.

You can map your data into the building blocks this way early in your streamlining development process based on initial interviews, or you can work out the details for surfacing and inventing processes through visioning and storyboarding, as described in the following chapter. Once you've walked through this process of supporting the work at the role, responsibility, and task level, you will have a design specification for your new composite application.

5.2.3 Context Maps

When introducing the information architecture of business applications at the beginning of this chapter, we described various archetypes of contextual work and presented different examples of UI building blocks that reflect a specific work context and enable users to act on it.

One very efficient way of getting from requirements to a first application structure is to identify all potential candidates for such a context and then list them together with some high-level descriptions as illustrated in the following table (see Figure 5.11).

Context	Views	Actions	Complex Actions
Requirements Management (Work Center)	• New Requirements • My Requirements • Change Notifications	• Collect Requirements • Update Requirements • Create Collection • Create Requirement • Subscribe to products and topics	• Explore Requirements Data Base • Organize Requirements and Structures • Compare Structures • Break Down Requirements
Single Requirement (Object Instance)	• Fact Sheet • Relationships • Specifications • Context Information	• Manage Attachments • Edit Values • Change Status	• Manage Relationships • Break Down
Requirements Structure (Object Instance)	• Fact Sheet • Relationships • Specifications • Context Information	• Manage Attachments • Manage Teams • Search Requirements • Insert Requirements	• Break Down • Compare Structures

Figure 5.11 Context Map for Selected Business Context in SAP xPD

Context maps describe key elements of business context:

▶ Type: Work Center, Object Instance, or ad-hoc Activity depending on the primary motivation for this context.

▶ Work-relevant *views* (aspects or perspectives) on the context enable users to understand the status of the corresponding work context.

▶ *Simple actions* are short-term tasks users want to perform within this context without leaving this context to accomplish goals.

▶ *Complex actions* need special attention, require some amount of time to finish, or are long-running and have their own persistence.

Identifying context maps is a rather straightforward process. As described earlier in this chapter, each organizational work role is clearly a candidate for a context map. Within each role, context-specific objects, actions, and views on the business are relevant. Each responsibility corresponds either to a view, an action, or a long-running activity that represents an activity that has its own persistence.

A process role points you to the process this role is participating in. If the role's task is only to the process standard workflow steps, those generated work items can be embedded into a Work Center in the form of work lists generated by the workflow.

If it feels like this is an activity initiated or managed by users, then it is worthwhile to model it as an independent context map reflecting all essential aspects of that activity. The same holds true for any business object that is part of your application. Depending on the role and the state of the object, available views and actions may differ.

Not only does differentiating between actions of different complexity help you to distinguish modeling as a contextual action instead of an independent activity, but, it also helps you to determine the appropriate position of these actions in the UI, which may be transient or persistent.

This may also influence the navigation behavior. Transient actions appear next to the contextual panel, while more complex activities that need to make apparent their own context may open as a new context window with its own contextual panel.

A complex action may be better modeled as a composite activity that needs some persistence for an extended length of time, because it requires multiple steps or careful consideration. For example, comparing product requirements with respect to conflicting or supporting items is not a simple action, but a complex task on which a user must focus for more than a second or two until the task is completed. If actions need their own context, you should describe them in a separate context map. As illustrated in Figure 5.12, you can get into a little more detail and include the purpose and key responsibilities so you don't lose track of the general design focus.

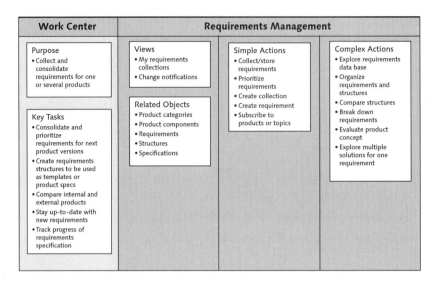

Figure 5.12 Example of Context Map for Requirements Management Work Center

Depending on the stage of your project, you may include even more details into a context map than shown in this figure. Once you have defined the essential elements of each context map, you can proceed and map the content to the appropriate contextual building blocks, such as a Work Center or an object instance view.

Having created this first design, you are now ready to create a mockup and test it with users, or you can refine the design further with additional details gathered through field interviews. We recommend that you mock up the design fairly quickly, before the entire application is specified completely. You can expect changes during the mock-up refinement process; so it's a good idea to start testing the "big picture" of your design before working on the details.

6 Creating and Iterating the Designs

UI building blocks are central to envisioning a new work practice for users and a new application design to support it. The consolidated models that we discussed in previous chapters enable the team to see existing work practice and to understand the intents behind the existing work practice at the user level and at the enterprise level. These insights and observations help to design a new solution that addresses business as well as individual needs. The new solution restructures the work practice and reengineers the business process with the help of UI building blocks.

Applications work best when they are designed from an understanding of how they can support a new way of working for the individual, the work group, and the business. Any application design benefits from developing a vision that describes the new work practice, considers how appropriate UI building blocks might be used, and decides what additional function and applications might be needed to best support the work. Depending on the type of project, this high-level vision can be detailed in storyboards or scenarios before mapping it to a particular UI design leveraging the UI building blocks. But no matter what type of project you are running—streamlining, surfacing, or invention—you want to be sure that the new system concept is tested with users and iterated until it meets their requirements.

In this chapter, we outline the steps of Contextual Design that can help your team produce a best-in-class application leveraging UI building blocks:

▶ **Visioning**

Designing the new work practice of the organization as it will be supported by the new system; created as a story by the entire team

▶ **Storyboarding**

Working out the details of the new work practice, step by step, using pictures augmented with text descriptions

▶ Paper Prototyping

Testing and iterating the new design on paper, with users, by mocking up their own work scenarios in a rough paper prototype of the new application

In addition to driving the design, the team needs to be able to communicate the design to stakeholders. We end this chapter by discussing the role of *personas*, *storyboards*, and *scenarios* in sharing the redesign concepts and creating buy-in with stakeholders and users. This is particularly important when developing applications for users internal to the business.

6.1 Visioning a Redesigned Process

As we've seen, the complexity of the project dictates the complexity of the process that is required to handle the problem. A simple streamlining project might be able to do much of this reinvention work through building and testing the building block design in paper prototypes of user interfaces. But surfacing and inventing projects affect the work practice more radically; the team needs processes to help them think about the impact of proposed changes. Furthermore, because any project is likely to have its unexpected problems, where what seemed well-understood turns out to require a new design, it's useful for everyone to understand the processes for working through that new design from user data as a team.

Visioning is the process that supports this design step. It allows a team to work together on redesigning the work practice, inventing system support as needed, using the UI building blocks. Contextual Design represents visions as drawings showing the story of users interacting with the proposed new system and how the work practice is transformed by the introduction of technology. A vision depicts how manual practices, human interactions, and tools come together with new application design to better support the whole practice. Visioning identifies needed function in the context of the larger work practice. This technique ensures that the team members postpone lower-level decisions about implementation, platform, and user interface until they have a clear picture of how their solution fits into the whole of the practice.

The primary intent of visioning is to redesign the work practice, not to design a user interface. Also, because a visioning session is a group activity, it fosters a shared understanding among team members and helps them to use their different points of view to push creativity.

Whether you're a team of two or six, the visioning process helps you work out the details of the new work practice for your users. It synthesizes design concepts into a new process that fits with the overall business process and the technical realities of the systems that will support it—be they legacy applications, new systems, or composite applications. If a project doesn't require much new work practice design, visions may simply give the team a way to lay out how the UI building blocks will be used to support the existing process. Streamlining projects are most likely to leave the basic structure of existing work practice unchanged, although for more complex projects, visioning at the task level ensures that the new design can support the existing process.

Visions can be "visionary" or follow the constraints of the existing business structure or technology. This decision is driven by the scope of the project, but it does not determine the level of innovation regarding the solution. The solution can be very innovative, even if traditional technology is used and vice versa. However, framing the vision by deciding about the vision scope increases efficiency and gets more buy-in from development.

Visioning need not be a time-consuming or complicated process. It's possible and appropriate to do a few quick visions in a couple of hours for a simpler project. After multiple visions, the team evaluates the options and synthesizes them into a single vision incorporating the best parts of each.

Throughout visioning and storyboarding (discussed in the next section), the team incorporates UI building blocks into their thinking. They use the vision and consolidated data to drive selecting appropriate building blocks, filling them out with appropriate work instances, and tailoring them to meet the needs of users and the business process. During visioning, the use of building blocks is just sketched out—the details will be filled in when storyboarding takes place. Visioning is best done when the major data collection has been completed and the results analyzed.

Visioning is a relatively simple team process that works well to synthesize ideas into a coherent whole. It can be combined with more formal presentations and working sessions, but for many projects, visioning is a process that works well.

The Visioning Session

The first step to a visioning session is to review each model and the affinity diagram, in turn, immersing the team in customer data so their designs are grounded in the users' work. Each designer or stakeholder starts by reviewing the data individually, generating design ideas, or envisioning new technology that better meets the needs of the users, the business process, and the organization. Team members compare ideas and begin to get a shared idea of how to respond to the data. This individual activity helps to stimulate general team discussion about the potential redesign, which prepares everyone for the visioning session itself.

Anyone involved in visioning should participate in "walking the data" that is usually hanging up on the wall of a team room. Without this "walk," the process is no longer data-driven; anyone could arrive and offer his or her favorite design ideas based on feelings and prejudices. Walking customer data results in the selection and tailoring of preexisting ideas to fit the needs of the population. Since the visioning process evaluates visions based, in part, on their fit to the data, knowing the data is important for anyone participating in the process.

The team also reviews the UI building blocks. Just as walking the data puts the customer data in the designers' head, reviewing the design patterns puts the technology in their head. When customer data and technological possibility come together in the head of a good designer, innovation happens.

To start the visioning session, the team picks a starting point and builds a story of the new work practice. A starting point may be the beginning of the known process, the story of one key member of a work group, or the story of a key task.

The team builds and draws the story on a flip chart, fitting ideas from each team member into the story as it unfolds. The story describes the new work practice, showing people, roles, systems, and anything else the vision requires. As the story touches each role and task, the team introduces appropriate UI building blocks; for example, when the user starts doing the work of a role, the team might introduce the Work Center building block to structure support for that role. The team does not worry about practicality at this point; all ideas are included.

During the vision and between visions, the team should ask itself whether it is accounting for all the data and design options it has available. Have all roles been considered? Are their key responsibilities and tasks well supported, with places in the design that allow the users to focus on the needs of that role or task? Have UI building blocks been used appropriately to organize and integrate the work of the different roles? Are there other designs, perhaps from previous projects in the organization, that should be considered and reused?

A team often generates several visions to cover all aspects of the problem and to drive its own creativity. The team may envision from multiple different assumptions how to restructure a work practice for increased efficiency or how to rely on increasingly leading-edge technology.

This results in a few (between three and five is good) visions for the team to work from. The team evaluates them with a simple process: for each vision, by first listing the good points—ways in which the vision supports the work practice or is easy to do organizationally or technically. Then the bad points are listed—ways in which the vision does not support users, depends on unrealistic technology, or is hard to do organizationally. While listing these problems, the team captures ideas to overcome these bad points. Finally, the team uses this evaluation to identify the best points of the different visions and synthesize them into one coherent work-practice solution.

Figure 6.1 shows an example from one of the vision sessions during which the team brainstormed how to support collection and evaluation of new product ideas. Instead of having one big pile of unsorted ideas, the system design helps to classify ideas and generate personalized inboxes for each product or topic owner based on personalization rules and role-based settings. For each of the ideas, the system offers the initiation of a standardized review process during which the ideas are assessed from various experts.

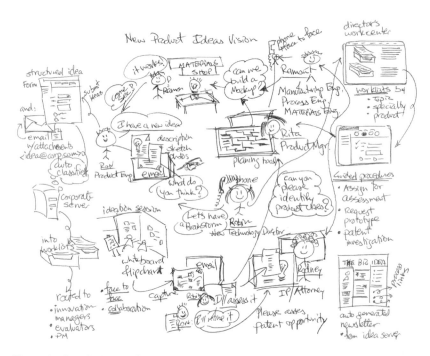

Figure 6.1 Sample Output from One of the Vision Sessions

6.2 Storyboarding the Details of the New Process

The consolidated vision represents a high-level idea of what the new system will be. To make it real, the team needs to work out the details—exactly what content will be available in which building blocks, what properties to expose, which values to watch in dashboards, and so on. *Storyboarding* or narrative scenarios is a way of working through these details that keeps work practice coherent without imposing a lot of process overhead. You need a story to test the flow of system interaction within and between building blocks.

Storyboards, like those used to plan a movie, combine pictures and text to describe the action. A storyboard cell is hand-drawn on a piece of paper (half sheets are about the right size) and depicts one step in the work practice. Some cells just show action between people; other cells show people interacting with the system being designed; and still others show what the system does internally to make user-visible behavior possible. The sketches are annotated with text to describe the action.

When a storyboard step shows the user interacting with the system, the interaction can use a UI building block. Where a building block exists to support the storyboard cell, designers sketch the building block and annotate it with the content the user needs at this point. Object instance views or Guided Procedure steps are sketched out in the action area of the building block. Where legacy systems provide a function that is embedded in the new system, those interfaces are sketched as they will appear in the new system.

Each storyboard describes one particular work situation or case. It shows how a task is accomplished following a particular strategy. If the task requires collaboration among multiple people or if it is handed off from person to person, one storyboard can describe the entire task. However, if you've observed two different strategies in your user population and the new design will support both, you need two storyboards—one for each strategy.

Storyboards are similar to midlevel use cases, focusing on the work steps of a task. But, unlike use cases, storyboards are pictorial—they allow designers to sketch out the interfaces they envision and embed those interfaces in the work practice they are designing. This ties together the whole user experience and supports the designers' need to see (literally) the system that they are creating. At the same time, the graphical nature of storyboards prevents the team from getting too detailed—complete specification of structure and function follows the step of working things out.

The steps and strategies of a work practice, being tacit, are easy to overlook. But sequence models capture the real moment-by-moment work activities. Working through detailed stories, guided by sequence consolidations and swim-lane diagrams, keeps the team honest and the design clean. Guided by the detailed models, the vision is made real. This ensures that the team does not overlook any intents and steps that are critical to the work. Even if the work is to be changed, the team has to think through the details of how it will be changed to ensure that adoption is easy.

Once the envisioned story and the set of building blocks are stabilized, you may capture the final version in the form of narrative scenarios that help you to test the flow of interaction. They also serve as use patterns for design sessions and usability testing. Such scenarios may be attached to personas to facilitate design sessions that should stay focused on real user needs.

6.3 Iterating Design

Regardless of project type, whether streamlining, surfacing, or inventing, each team must test the proposed user interface and overall system design. Managing risk means ensuring that the design works for the people and the business process, and is bought into by the people who will be using the application. Mock-up testing is the best way to simultaneously test the design, discover overlooked functions, and involve stakeholders in co-creating the final solution. For product companies, iteration of the design finalizes the requirements, tests the design for its use across companies, and generates sales excitement among customers. No matter what the project type, mock-up testing is critical to a team's success.

Even when based on data, the design is actually a theory about how users can work better. To find out if this theory is correct, it must be tested—and it can be tested only with the people who will use it. But users—business workers—are not data modelers or systems designers. They do not understand the implications of an object model or a flow model on their own work practice. They cannot even articulate their work practice because it is tacit, so how can they tell if changes to the system and their work practice will work?

An accurate test of the new application depends on a representation of the system that users can both understand *and* interact with. This means the team must represent their ideas as a user interface. Mock-up testing lets users interact with user interface prototypes as though they were real. Users can provide reliable feedback on whether they like the work practice that results. During the mock-up interview, the designer can get feedback on low-level details of the system design that would be very difficult to confirm in any other way.

Low-Fidelity Prototype Testing

The fastest and most efficient way to build the first system prototype is in paper, using normal stationary supplies. Card stock provides a stable background to simulate the screen. Sticky notes effectively simulate anything that might be moved during an interview, such as menus, dialogs, or buttons. Sample content is put on a removable sheet so that users can replace it with their own, real content during the interview. Designs that include new hardware can use other kinds of props to simulate devices, robots, panel interfaces, and whatever else is needed. The final prototype may be rough, but it represents both the system's structure and its behavior.

Figure 6.2 shows an example of a low-fidelity paper prototype illustrating the idea of organizing requirements within the SAP xPD Work Center. Similar mock-ups along with other pieces were presented to the users who pretended to use it for their real work. Changes to the design were made in the moment in response to issues. This process was used to reveal insights about what functionality is needed for an efficient management of requirements and how users wanted to organize their buckets of requirements, e.g. personal collections vs. formal requirements structures.

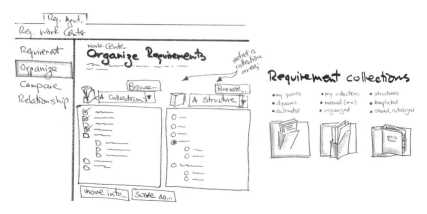

Figure 6.2 Example of Low-Fidelity Paper Prototype for Requirements Within Management Work Center

Mock-up interviews help designers understand why design elements work or fail and help identify new functions. These interviews are based on the principles of Contextual Interviews that we described earlier. The team tests the paper prototype with users in their own context to keep them grounded in their real work practice. Users interact with the prototype by writing in their own content and by manipulating and modifying the prototype. The partnership is one of codesign — as users work with the prototype following a task they need to do or did in the recent past, the user and interviewer uncover problems and in real time, they change the prototype to fix them. Together the user and interviewer interpret what is going on in the usage and come up with alternative designs instantiated in paper. Hand-drawn paper prototypes make it clear to the user that icons, layout, and other interface details are not central to the purpose of the interviews. Because the prototypes are rough, they keep the user focused on testing structure and function.

The mock-up interview is a field interview, but is conducted by two people. One team member manipulates the prototype, presenting new screens as needed by the task that the user is performing. The other person takes detailed notes of what is touched or changed, as well as the overall response to the prototype. The interpretation session captures issues and changes to each screen at the level of function, interaction design, and overall usability. The team pays special attention to whether UI building blocks are really working or need to be extended, to the support for collaboration and workflow, and to whether the full task activities and data needs are being addressed.

After the team tests and interprets the prototype with three to four users, the team redesigns it to respond to the feedback. Multiple rounds of interviews and iterations allow testing in increasing levels of detail, first addressing structural issues, then, user interface theme and layout issues, and finally, detailed user interaction issues. Over the multiple rounds, the application is tested with all the different roles that will use it. Before stabilizing the requirements and design of the system, we recommend three rounds of iteration with each business role that the system is supposed to support.

6.4 Visioning and Prototyping for Different Kinds of Projects

The kind of project you have affects how you use visioning, storyboarding, and prototyping. Here are some ideas for tweaking the process based on your project type:

Surfacing and *inventing* projects benefit from running visioning sessions after consolidating requirements and building an affinity diagram. Inventing projects, because of their wide impact, may run multiple visioning sessions with different stakeholders in the project. This is a useful way to get organizational buy-in, including buy-in from the client organization that has to adopt the change. By seeing and contributing to early ideas, the client organization's task of introducing the new application becomes much easier. Product groups need to convince their development organizations to take a new direction—not only management and marketing, but also the teams working on related products.

The team should test their new design with paper mockups, using several rounds to incorporate feedback and flesh out the design. Once the design has stabilized, the team can move on to visual design and implementation. If they can generate a running prototype or HTML mockup, the design will benefit from additional Contextual Interviews with key users to catch low-level interaction and usability issues. And if the team can implement a working version on top of the underlying technology, then performance, real data lookup, and links can be tested.

Working with your users throughout the development cycle for any composite application project ensures that the function and layout is working at every level of detail. As always, more work with the user population ensures greater buy-in as the team expands the numbers of users interviewed with each round of iteration.

Streamlining projects can move directly from initial prototype (developed through the direct UI mapping process described in Section 3.2.3) to prototype iterations, but they can benefit from lightweight visioning and storyboarding to develop the initial prototype. More complex streamlining projects should at least storyboard the new work practice to ensure that the UI building blocks do indeed cover the activities of the necessary tasks. Market research and data from the initial interviews form the source data for the vision and storyboards. The "plusses-and-minuses" process helps the team weed out the weak ideas and develop a more robust design. Reviewing of storyboards by potential users provides high-level feedback and increases buy-in.

A streamlining project can start prototyping immediately. With only a few Contextual Interviews and initial analysis to flesh out the UI building blocks needed, the team has a reasonable cut at a workable system. During the first iteration, the team must stay vigilant, looking for new practice and different ways of approaching existing practice than was anticipated during the brief initial analysis.

For streamlining projects, we recommend starting with a standard Contextual Interview to get an overview of the users' work process and ensure that it does indeed map reasonably well to the mock-up as planned. If the interviewer finds the user going beyond the work practice as understood, he may need to expand this portion of the interview by collecting standard Contextual Interview data. As the interviewer understands how to modify the mockup in order to incorporate the unexpected work practice, the mockup is introduced and the interviewer makes the necessary changes in real time. If the work practice is too different (or the interviewer is less conversant with UI building blocks), the data can be brought back to the team for consideration, consolidation, and redesign.

If the new work practice is well-supported by the mockup, the interviewer simply moves to the standard mock-up interview. In any situation where a new work practice appears, if the interviewer can identify an existing UI building block that could support it, he may sketch a prototype on the fly and revise it with the user.

6.5   Communicating a Design

In real organizations, no project team works in a vacuum. They must coordinate with other teams and gain approval from management. Communicating the proposed design clearly is one of a team's most important tasks.

Because any design process creates tangible artifacts throughout, it's generally straightforward to build communications describing a design. Here are some methods we've found to be useful:

▶ The *vision* is the team's high-level statement of what the design is and how it affects the work. Not only does it keep various members of the team working toward the same goal, it helps communicate to project stakeholders. When summarized with data and displayed as a slide show, the vision communicates the redesign intention and shows how UI building blocks can be leveraged for significant change. Internal projects can show the client organization what they are getting and how it will affect them, producing buy-in and getting feedback on the design. Product developers can show marketing what the product will do, both for buy-in and for preselling to customer prospects. The vision shows developers what will be required of them so they can start investigating technology issues. For management, the team can show what is being created and why there is a need for it. At this point in the process, many teams organize sharing events to communicate the status and direction of their work.

▶ *Storyboards* are a convenient way of describing and communicating the new work practice, because they walk through the user's work as a coherent process and integrate UI sketches into the work. The team can walk the storyboard with stakeholders to show what the new system delivers and how it works; this raises understanding and acceptance among those who are not appropriate candidates for prototype interviews.

▶ *Personas* and *scenarios* are ways to describe "typical" users so that those unfamiliar with the data have a concrete representation of their users. The consolidated flow model provides all the information required for robust personas. First, you identify core users of the proposed system and note their principal roles from the flow models. Then, you look across the range of users studied and build representative users drawing on those key roles. The roles show their intents, their tasks, and their concerns; building these characteristics into the personas results in a robust representation of the different user archetypes that you want to support.

Scenarios describe how these personas work in the context of different tasks and work situations. They describe the "to-be" work practice, building in the work practice designed in the vision. Each scenario illustrates a key work situation and shows how the different personas work alone or together to get the work accomplished.

Scenarios are built from the vision and storyboards. They describe the sequence of work steps and handoffs between people defined by the storyboard. Like a storyboard, each scenario focuses on a single task and work situation (for example, driving a modification of an existing product versus inventing a product). Scenarios work best with personas to provide an easy-to-follow description of who the users are and how they will work.

Product Manager	
Needs	▶ Database with product requirements and market data
	▶ Portfolio tools to oversee product innovation efforts
	▶ Planning tools for managing product changes
Goals	▶ Make sure that no cool idea is lost
	▶ Drive innovation at reasonable costs and efforts

Table 6.1 Example of a Persona-Like Description of a Product Manager

Personas, scenarios, and storyboards are good communication devices. Slide shows embodying the vision and the initial data also help communicate the team's direction. Put personas on posters; take digital photos of the storyboard frames and display them in slides for stakeholders to review. Because scenarios tell the detailed story of the user's interaction with the system in an accessible form, potential users and business stakeholders can understand the proposed process and provide feedback. This is especially useful for internal teams to generate buy-in.

7 Making Innovation Happen

Real innovation comes from understanding the users' current work practice, the organization's business goals in redesigning or inventing a new practice, and the underlying technology that must be used to support the work. System design is always about work practice design, because systems exist to support how we do things. But getting it right is hard if you don't have the tools to understand the work or an underlying technology designed to help support it.

Composite applications built on top of the SAP NetWeaver platform are unique, because the platform generates superior user experience and business process support through its UI building blocks. Armed with data from the techniques of Contextual Design about how your users work, you can design new applications that streamline existing work processes, surface and automate hidden processes, and invent new processes to support evolving challenges of the business. Data drives every dimension of innovation: process, work practice, and change management. And innovation can be deliberately designed at every layer of our innovation cube in Chapter 1 (see Figure 1.1).

But innovation is not just about understanding users and designing what works for them and the business. Innovation is dependent on the organization adopting the changed business practices and using the systems that support them. Too often, IT organizations investigate new technologies, build prototype systems, try them out with a pilot group—often the IT department itself—and then start rolling it out to the larger organization. New technology, even SAP NetWeaver technology, cannot by itself ensure that users use the software. UI building blocks, even those designed initially with user data, cannot ensure that the way they are designed and rolled out for your organization will work for your users. As we've discussed in this book, deliberate design and iteration of business processes and systems—combined with a user-centered design process—are what ensure success. Success is measured not only in the creation of an innovative system or a better process; success includes successful employee adoption, smooth change management, *and* systems that delight the users while supporting new business processes.

In this chapter, we describe ways to drive innovation. First, we tell you how to define projects to increase significant innovation. Then, we discuss how user-centered design techniques increase the probability of user adoption.

7.1 Innovating the Business Process: Shifting Scope

Some organizations are looking for significant innovation, while other organizations simply want to put in needed processes or streamline what is already there. Regardless of the chosen means of innovation, all successful innovation is driven by understanding the users' work practice; if you let user data drive the design, how you define the project and who you talk to will determine the issues you surface to address. Therefore, the scope of your innovation is ultimately determined by the project scope you define and the data you choose to collect.

Once you understand that, you can choose the level and degree of innovation that is appropriate for your situation. Although government, law, or cultural trends may cause you to make changes from the outside, you can drive the innovation directly. By changing your definition of the problem, you can open up the possibilities of how to run your business.

7.1.1 Expand Your Scope of Innovation

The nature and scope of the innovation depends on the scope of the project. If you choose a streamlining project, you are choosing stepwise change to the existing practice by introducing technology. If you choose a surfacing project, you are choosing to put structure into processes that you know are supporting the business but that are currently not formally defined. Because a surfacing project does not yet have defined procedures, you have an opportunity to redesign your processes and investigate new technologies. An inventing project recognizes from the beginning that the goal of design is to disrupt normal practice or institute a new required practice. An inventing project will, by definition, shift culture, roles, responsibilities, and technology.

When you choose the type of project you plan to do, you automatically choose how much innovation you are willing to take on.

But, as we have said, successful design at any level requires modeling the work of real people doing real work. If you want to see issues, root causes, and best practices, go out into the field and understand the formal or informal business process; the tasks, communication, coordination, and self-organization of people in the core work group; and the way technology is used to support or hinder the work. You will also naturally see opportunity for change beyond the innovation scope you selected. The consolidated field data and the work models present you with an opportunity to expand your scope of innovation. If you choose to redesign to this expanded scope, you will introduce more change and innovation into your project. For example:

▶ A streamlining project focuses on eliminating pain points, overcoming breakdowns, reducing steps of inefficient processes, and automating activities that can be taken over by systems. But the field data for a streamlining project may also reveal unsurfaced procedures, collaborations, information needs, and the way workers get around the formal process to make it work. If you expand your scope to improve the process by defining and supporting unsurfaced activities, you will start to support the work more directly.

▶ A surfacing project can be achieved only when hidden processes are identified and mapped. Modeling the real work process allows organizations to make decisions about how they want to work once they see what they are actually doing. Real workflow can be defined, roles and responsibilities can be negotiated, tasks can be streamlined or eliminated, online artifacts can be created to replace paper, and collaborative environments can be implemented to bring people and information together. But a surfacing project also shows where the unsurfaced process touches formal processes and integrates people, data, and activities across formal processes. You can expand your scope to include redesigning the system of processes that work together to have a greater impact on the efficiency of your business.

▶ An inventing project starts with modeling the business as it is and then understanding how it can be changed. When inventing, there's no existing "best practice" to be studied—the new practice will become the next "best practice." But all new processes may have analogs in existing processes implemented in organizations. For example, the need to monitor and report on a new environmental substance for the government is similar to monitoring and reporting on other work conditions for which data and best practice do exist. Moving from an in-house innovation team to co-invention with open-source communities can be informed by studying collaboration with any distributed group or existing open-source community. An inventing project can collect data and best-practice information on analogous processes to find ideas that work for the new process. Borrowing good ideas from related practices is the cornerstone of innovative redesign.

Whatever the original scope of your project, you can choose more or less innovation by increasing the scope to include those areas revealed by the data you have collected. Or, you can collect additional data that will give you new ideas for innovation gathered from analogous processes. Even if you lack the time to address all that you discover in the existing project, you now know where to take your next inquiry to make a real impact on the way you do business.

7.1.2   Look Beyond Your Targeted Business Scenario

No innovation is ever totally disconnected from what has gone on before. Process redesign changes how people work by introducing technology, by changing roles and responsibilities, and by changing how tasks are accomplished. Redesign can introduce change at the level of the individual activity, the work group, the department, or the business process. But all redesign emanates from how the project is defined and bounded.

Next-practice design comes from changing your point of view when redesigning a business process. Consider the difference in business process redesign from within the following business boundaries:

▶ **Challenge the Department**

When a department models the work of its employees, it streamlines and surfaces practices occurring within the boundaries of the department. The background assumption is that the work of the department itself is fixed and delivers optimum value to the business. Insofar as the department is part of a larger corporate business process, this departmental redesign does not challenge the role of the department or allow for achieving the work of the larger business process differently or more directly.

Innovation is expanded when you allow yourself to challenge the role of the department and how the rest of the business is supported to achieve the overall business intent—not the espoused intent that brought the department into existence. Maybe there is another, better way to achieve the business goal if you look deeply into how and why the work proceeds as it does.

▶ **Challenge the Business Model**

When a business models the work of its business from within the boundaries of the company, it optimizes the business's current relationship to customers, vendors, and partners. It sees its business process in terms of internal reorganization. It may seek to optimize its relationship to customers, vendors, and partners, but it maintains its integrity as a separate business. However, if you expand the boundary of the problem to include how you work with other businesses and organization, you may redefine your relationship to your partners and surface new services you can provide.

Business and work practices that cross traditional process boundaries are ideally situated for composite application development. For example, manufacturers and retailers are currently undergoing a revolution in inventory management relationships with their suppliers, with practices such as vendor-managed inventory and supplier-managed inventory. Consumer packaged goods manufacturers like

Procter & Gamble must manage inventory on Wal-Mart store shelves within tight target minimum and maximum stock levels or risk stiff penalties. Many departments—sales, demand management, supply chain planning, and finance, to name just a few—are affected. An IT platform, such as SAP NetWeaver, can enable the business to redefine their processes on a continuous base.

▶ **Challenge the Enterprise**
Many of the most powerful approaches to inventing new processes come from treating the entire enterprise as just another silo—one function within the larger virtual organization that consists of suppliers, subcontractors, and delivery channels all working together to provide customer value. When the scope of a process is widened to include all the partners and collaborators in an industry, the role of each type of business—indeed the entire way in which products and services are created and delivered—can be challenged.

This scope of the entire value network allows for the invention of new businesses or new processes, redistribution of work across companies, outsourcing of work, and using resources in a distributed fashion across the globe. The auto industry is a good example of continuous redefinition of its business processes from the point of view of collaboration among businesses.

No matter how you define the scope of your problem, the tools of modeling work based on real field data allow you to see what is going on. You can then apply new business models, technology, and processes to the work of creating business value. Change in scope alters what will be invented. New process design comes from widening the scope of redesign beyond the traditional scope, challenging "business as usual."

7.1.3 Change Your Redesign Perspective

Widening scope to consider larger chunks of the business is one way to drive new process design. Changing the perspective from which you redesign also produces innovation. Consider the following cases:

▶ **Enabling the Individual**

The human resources department has services that it provides the employee. The management team has messages it wants to deliver to the employee. Redesign from the departmental perspective creates pockets of information and services. But shifting from a departmental perspective to an employee perspective changes the point of view of redesign. The employee experiences one relationship to the business as a whole. From the employee's perspective, all information, services, messages, and activities relevant to all their job activities should be brought together. By taking the employee's perspective, a business can optimize how it communicates to and services the employee. Departments fade from view and the needs of the employee dominate.

For example, from the perspective of the business process, people may participate inside one process. But managers at every level participate in many business processes. Optimizing work at the level of the business process can fragment the work of the manager. Redesign from the managers' perspective brings all the relevant parts of their world together—cutting across all business processes. Business process recedes from the focus. The overview and tasks of the manager dominate.

▶ **Enabling Process Roles**

People have job titles that are supposed to imply the work they do. These job titles are used by IT to deploy functions to employees based on role templates. However, job titles don't map cleanly to what people really do. The secretary becomes the forms maker for the company. The sales man is also the sales trainer because she happens to be good at the job. The manager is also the project leader because the group is small. The CEO of the small company is also the key marketer. Job titles don't reflect the real process roles that people play in the organization. Moreover, people's daily tasks are determined by the actual activities in which they are engaged. Many years of field data collection across enterprises reveals that job title is not an appropriate way to think about supporting the work of the organization.

If you look beyond job titles and understand the roles and responsibilities in a given work situation, you'll see how to make the process more efficient and enable the individual to be productive at the same time. You will generate new ideas of how to support individuals to manage a multitude of processes and contribute to their larger work situations.

▶ Enabling Management Initiative

A business process typically involves a standard way of doing a core business activity. Business process reengineering involves changing or revealing that standard process to optimize it. An initiative driven from upper levels of management operates outside of normal business process, even as it drives tasks into it. An initiative might change the core mission of the company to open new markets, change the culture to radically increase productivity, or change sales and marketing strategies to reach out to and relate to customers and partners in new ways. It generates activities, investigations, information needs, and visibility needs that are both vertical and horizontal, occurring within and outside existing business processes.

Redesign to support management initiatives requires understanding what needs to be monitored, tracked, and managed—looking beyond standard process management tools.

▶ Enabling the Work Group

Business process looks at the flow of work throughout the company. Individual work is seen as happening at the desktop. But most business work is collaborative. Management work groups of strategists, managers, and administrators oversee company activity. Teams deliver products. Informal groups of colleagues from a profession within and outside the company build knowledge of new techniques and approaches. This new knowledge is fed back into project work. Individual collaboration across companies makes corporate collaboration work. Too often we redesign to optimize the work of business processes or individuals, but ignore the work group—the core social element that moves production forward in any company.

Innovation can come simply by shifting your scope, your perspective, and the data you gather. A shift in focus lets you see what else you can address that is revealed in the data you collect, as well as pointing you to new data that you might collect. If you have the data and a model of what is actually going on in your organization, you can choose how much or how little to address. But, without the data, you lose the opportunity for a greater impact on your organization.

Redesign with the help of a flexible technology like the SAP business process platform can drive real process invention and redesign of practices. Once you know what you want to build, you can take advantage of the service-oriented architecture (SOA) and the generic building blocks that can deliver process changes to the desktops of users quickly. You will also know what you need to build uniquely to complete your new vision. As you ship these new technologies that now embody your process and user redesigned practices, you will create a natural feedback loop for continuous process and system improvement. If enterprises have technology supporting clearly defined process, they can indeed manage their processes deliberately by putting metrics in place to help gauge effectiveness and adoption.

7.2   Organizational Adoption: Creating Buy-In

Once the business changes and associated systems have been designed and iterated with users, you are ready to build and roll them out to the organization. Any process or system change means organizational change as well and needs to be introduced into the culture. Procedures must change to match the new goals and new business structure; people must adapt to new roles and expectations; and the culture of the business itself may need to shift to accommodate new business goals. But often users are simply not cooperative. Why don't people adopt the new systems that are supposed to help them work?

Transforming organizational processes and their supporting systems is a challenge for any organization. The task can seem overwhelming—from the initial definition of scope to the final design of new roles, responsibilities, procedures, systems, and user interfaces. Getting it right for the people, the business, and the budget, while managing internal politics, organizational adoption, and reliable implementation can be a daunting task.

The Contextual Design techniques we have outlined in this book help you design the right thing while gathering buy-in. How?

▶ **Field Data**

When you go to the real users of the system in your target market or internal organization, you will watch what they do and listen to what they say. You will understand the real practice and real requirements. Gathering data from the business creates a "listening" process that assures people their point of view has been heard.

▶ **Systemic Approach**

When you model the whole work and vision a coherent solution, you ensure that your new business process and technology solution will work for the people within it. But if you artificially break the problem or the solution into parts that will have to be re-synthesized later, you are less likely to develop a process that actually works. If you invent by forming subteams to model and redesign processes, investigate and select system platforms, and design the user experience, you are less likely to develop a process that actually works. If you list features as a way of making decisions about software to build or acquire—without having a clear understanding of how the system fits into the work—you are less likely to develop a process that actually works. And if you reinvent roles and responsibilities without considering how that impacts potential automation, end users, informal work practice, and the overall efficiency of the business process, you're less likely to develop a process that actually works. Modeling and visioning naturally synthesize all these perspectives and produce a high-level view of where the organization can go.

▶ **Iteration with Users**

When you test the design with real users in the field and iterate the design with the real users, you generate buy-in with the people who will use the system, because they're involved in creating it. You will be able to simulate roles, responsibilities, and new procedures that are introduced by your new composite application. The whole socio-technical system can be designed, tested, and redesigned with the people who will use them. People feel that they are part of the process, instead of feeling like their corporation is imposing change upon them.

▶ **Continuous Communication Out**
When you work with people, they feel heard. When you continuously present your understanding to people as well, you keep them in the loop – and they feel heard. You can use the artifacts of Contextual Design to create slideshows, articulate the vision, share storyboards, and reveal the user interface so that everyone knows what is happening.

Because users are involved in the design process and the actual design, they can see the emerging changes. There are no surprises. Buy-in comes from involvement and is helped by road shows that keep everyone informed all along the process. Involvement is a natural part of a user-centered design process. Issues of user adoption within organizations become manageable, thereby making you more successful.

When a user-centered design process is combined with a business process platform that is optimized to support real people and real processes, successful innovation is possible. You *can* deliberately create business value if you have a technology and a design process that put understanding what people and businesses need in the center of the design process. With the SAP NetWeaver platform and Contextual Design, you can reinvent your business.

A Appendix: At-a-Glance Design Activities

Process Step	Description	Streamlining	Surfacing	Inventing
Project Scoping	Review innovation of new application idea	Review existence of processes and systems	Review existence of processes and systems	Review existence of processes, systems, external requirements
Problem Analysis	Initial investigation of the market space: investigate best practices, market expectations, business expectations, and competition	Document high-level view of standard process and pain points from internal documents and key stakeholders	Basic investigation: for internal projects, traditional interviews with stakeholder to set focus and generate buy-in	Basic investigation, especially of best practices: discuss business goals with management stakeholders to clarify productivity or legal expectations
Initial Prototype	Create initial design to illustrate benefit based on UI building blocks, driven by some field data	Map ideas to UI building blocks to develop a first cut at the design for testing	As needed for creating a business case	As needed for creating a business case
Contextual Interviews	Conduct 1-on-1 field interviews with key users in their workplace, observing and talking about how they do the tasks the application is going to support		Conduct at least 4 field interviews with each primary participant in the business process to be supported	Conduct at least 4 field interviews with each primary participant in the business process to be supported, and at least 2 field interviews with secondary participants

Process Step	Description	Streamlining	Surfacing	Inventing
Interpretation and Data Modeling	Carry out group analysis of interview findings, capturing key issues and appropriate work models		Capture issues, building flow and sequence models for primary members of the work group to be supported	Capture issues, building flow and sequence models for primary and secondary members of the work group; optionally, use additional work models to capture cultural, physical distribution issues, and artifacts to be created or redesigned
Consolidation	Bring individual data together to show implications for market or business population		Build affinity and consolidate roles and processes in form of swim-lane diagrams	Build affinity, consolidate all models, and consolidate lower-level detail for tasks with no support in existing SAP xApp design patterns
Visioning	Walk the consolidated data defining key issues, work groups to be supported, and appropriate SAP xApp design patterns to build on. Create high-level view of how people will work in the future with the new system		Refine product vision and map requirements to appropriate building blocks; identify areas for new development if necessary	Vision the new process incorporating SAP xApp design patterns where appropriate

Process Step	Description	Streamlining	Surfacing	Inventing
Mapping to Building Blocks and UI Design	Work out stories of use in the new system guided by the consolidated data, the vision; define contextual maps and map them to design patterns		Build scenarios based on swim-lane diagrams; define contextual maps and identify appropriate UI building blocks to support the scenario	Build storyboards based on all consolidated data; define contextual maps and identify appropriate UI building blocks to support the scenario; create new designs where needed
Paper Prototyping	Mock up design in paper and iterate with users; start with Contextual Interviews as needed (3 rounds of mock-up interviews with key users in the work group to be supported)	Start with combined field interviews and mock-up testing; second and subsequent rounds of interviews focus on prototype iteration only	Conduct interviews with focus on prototype testing and redesign	Conduct interviews with focus on prototype testing and redesign

B   Sources And Further Reading

▶ Hugh Beyer and Karen Holtzblatt, *Contextual Design: Defining Customer-Centered Systems*. Morgan Kaufmann Publishers, Inc., San Francisco 1997.

▶ Karen Holtzblatt, Jessamyn Burns Wendell, Shelley Wood: *Rapid Contextual Design: A How-to Guide to Key Techniques for User-Centered Design*. Morgan Kaufmann Publishers, Inc., San Francisco 2004.

▶ Dan Woods: *Packaged Composite Applications: An O'Reilly Field Guide to Enterprise Software*. O'Reilly & Associates, Sebastopol 2003.

▶ W. Edwards Deming: *Out of Crisis*. Massachusetts Institute of Technology Center for Advanced Engineering Study, 1982.

C   About the Authors

Jörg Beringer, Director of User Experience of Emerging Solutions, SAP Labs, Palo Alto

Jörg leads the user experience group of Emerging Solutions, an innovative development organization at SAP Labs, Palo Alto. The group is focused on new emergent trends in business applications. Jörg joined SAP in 1997 and became responsible for managing strategic design projects within the EnjoySAP initiative. After establishing user centered design as part of SAP's best practices in requirements engineering, he moved to the Enterprise Portal group where he specialized in user productivity and work group support in business applications.

Jörg currently manages the user experience design group supporting xApps—SAP's first generation of composite applications. In his architectural role, Jörg is committed to promoting new ideas and innovative solutions for frameworks that improve the user experiences in business applications.

Jörg holds a PhD in Cognitive Psychology, from Technical University in Darmstadt.

Karen Holtzblatt, CEO and Co-founder of InContext and Contextual Design

Karen is the visionary behind InContext's unique customer-centered design approach, Contextual Design. Karen's combination of technological and psychological expertise provides the creative framework for driving the development, innovative designs, and design processes.

Recognized as a leader in the design community, Karen has pioneered transformative ideas and design approaches throughout her career. At Digital Equipment Corporation, Karen introduced Contextual Inquiry—the industry standard for gathering field data to understand how technology impacts the way people work. Contextual Inquiry and the design processes based on it provide a revolutionary approach for designing new products and systems based on a deep understanding of the context of use. Contextual Inquiry forms the base of Contextual Design, InContext's full customer-centered design process.

Karen co-founded InContext Enterprises in 1992 to use Contextual Design techniques to coach product teams and deliver customer-centered designs to businesses across multiple industries. The books, *Contextual Design: Defining Customer-Centered Systems,* and, most recently, *Rapid Contextual Design,* are used by companies and universities all over the world. InContext's CDTools™ product, launched in 2004, is the first tool suite to support teams doing customer-centered design. Karen's extensive experience with teams and all types of work and life practice underlies the innovation and reliable quality consistently delivered by InContext's teams.

Karen also has more than 20 years of teaching experience, professionally and in university settings. She holds a doctorate in applied psychology from the University of Toronto.

Index

**Leverage the value of
your business with
SAP's new infrastructure**

**Acquire unparalleled insights
from four exclusive
sample case studies**

312 pp., 2005, US$ 69.95
ISBN 1-59229-041-8

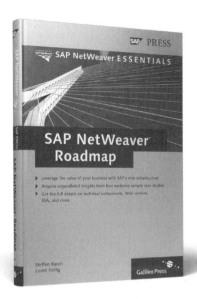

SAP NetWeaver Roadmap

S. Karch, L. Heilig, C. Bernhardt, A. Hardt,
F. Heidfeld, R. Pfennig

SAP NetWeaver Roadmap

This book helps you understand each of SAP
NetWeaver's components and illustrates, using
practical examples, how SAP NetWeaver, and its
levels of integration, can be leveraged by a wide
range of organizations.

Readers benefit from in-depth analysis featuring four
actual case studies from various industries, which
describe in detail how integration with SAP Net-
Weaver can contribute to the optimization of a
variety of essential business processes and how the
implementation works. Finally, detailed coverage of
SAP NetWeaver technology gives you the complete
picture in terms of architecture and functionality of
each component.

>> www.sap-press.de/955

Gain first insights into the Composite Application Framework

293 pp., 2005, with CD, 69,95 Euro
ISBN 1-59229-048-5

SAP xApps and the Composite Application Framework

www.sap-press.com

J. Weilbach, M. Herger

SAP xApps and the Composite Application Framework

This book provides you with a detailed introduction to all of the SAP components that are relevant to xApps, especially the integrated SAP NetWeaver tools (Composite Application Framework – CAF) for creating and customizing your own xApps. This unparalleled reference contains exclusive information, practical examples, and a wealth of screen shots from the CAF, taken from actual pilot projects. In addition, you'll uncover the ins and outs of SAP partner programs for developing and certifying your own xApps, and lots more.

>> www.sap-press.de/1017

Collaborative Processes, Interfaces, Messages, Proxies, and Mappings

Runtime, configuration, cross-component processes, and Business Process Management

Incl. technical case scenarios on cross-component BPM and B2B- Communication

270 pp., 2005, US$
ISBN 1-59229-037-X

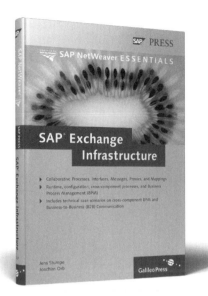

SAP Exchange Infrastructure

www.sap-press.com

J. Stumpe, J. Orb

SAP Exchange Infrastructure

If you know what SAP Exchange Infrastructure (SAP XI) is, and you have seen the latest documentation, then now you will want to read this book. Exclusive insights help you go beyond the basics, and provide you with in-depth information on the SAP XI architecture, which in turn helps you quickly understand the finer points of mappings, proxies, and interfaces. You'll also benefit from practical guidance on the design and configuration of business processes. Additionally, in a significant section devoted to step-by-step examples, you'll discover the nuances of various application scenarios and how to tackle their specific configurations.

>> www.sap-press.de/934

Technical principles, installation, programming of SAP EP 5.0 and 6.0

Content Integration with SAP BW, mySAP CRM, and ready-made iViews

310 pp., 2005, with CD, US$ 69.95
ISBN 1-59229-018-3

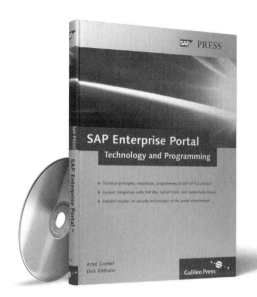

SAP Enterprise Portal

www.sap-press.com

A. Goebel, D. Ritthaler

SAP Enterprise Portal

Technology and programming

This book is a complete overview for the installation, operation and administration of a SAP-company portal (EP 6.0). Learn all there is to know about system requirements and the establishment of the portal in the system landscape. Get a step-by-step guide to the installation of a test system and discover how to adapt the portal to the requirements of the user and how to define roles.

The book focuses very much on content and application integration. You learn how to program Web-services and Portal-iViews, plus all there is to know about Unifer, and by use of the SAP Business Information Warehouse you get in-depth knowledge on content-integration.

>> www.sap-press.de/620